FRANCHISING

The Wiley Small Business Series

For the small business owner, success or failure often depends on the day-to-day management of hundreds of business problems and details. Drawing on the knowledge and experience of experts, these concise, detailed handbooks offer you sound advice and vital practical help on every aspect of managing a small business—sales, financing, accounting, advertising, security, and taxes—everything you need to operate a successful business. Look for them in your favorite bookstore.

Other Titles in the Series

*Forthcoming

FRANCHISING

William L. Siegel

A WILEY PRESS BOOK

John Wiley & Sons, Inc.
New York   Chichester   Brisbane   Toronto   Singapore

Publisher: Judy V. Wilson
Editor: Alicia Conklin
Managing Editor: Maria Colligan
Composition and Make-up: Cobb/Dunlop, Inc.

Library of Congress Cataloging in Publication Data

Siegel, William Laird.
  Franchising.

  (Wiley small business series)
  Includes index.
  1. Franchises (Retail trade) 2. Small
business. I. Title. II. Series.
HF5429.23.S57 1982   658.8'708   82-21951
  ISBN 0-471-09965-1 (pbk.)

Printed in the United States of America
83 84 10 9 8 7 6 5 4 3 2 1

Contents

FRANCHISING

Introduction

FRANCHISING COMMANDS a healthy share of American business. Nearly 1500 companies offer almost 500,000 franchises. More than 4 million people are employed by franchise operations, and almost a third of all retail sales are claimed by franchises. Many people earn a very comfortable living through franchising, and many happy Americans swear by franchising as a sure-fire way to reclaim the American dream.

Franchising has had its rough times, though. During the boom years of the fifties and sixties, franchising was often touted as a surefire method of getting rich. For many it was. But for some unlucky people it was a disaster. Shady or slipshod operators ruined a number of investors through dishonesty or sheer incompetence. The government ultimately intervened and passed laws to protect consumers from poorly set-up franchises or out-and-out frauds. Franchising underwent a baptism of fire and emerged stronger than ever.

Today franchising is highly respectable. Banks and other investors understand and appreciate the solidity of many franchising operations. In today's uncertain economy, people are searching for security. They are looking for a Gibralter to shelter them from inflation, recession, and abrupt economic shifts. Their big problem is where to look.

One solution, which is also the dream of many Americans, is to own a small business. But small businesses are failing right and left. The government estimates that 80 percent of small businesses fail within the first 3 years of operation. And how do you get the money to start a profitable business today? The likelihood of a bank providing novices with tens of thousands of dollars to start their own businesses is roughly like finding the Holy Grail.

One of the main roadblocks to obtaining a loan is that a fledgling businessperson often lacks the skill and experience it takes to get a concern off the ground. Starting a new business, as banks recognize and statistics verify, is not for everyone. There are literally hundreds of problems to deal with. Many things can go wrong, and if you're unprepared the result can be bankruptcy.

Yet there is a way to get an edge in the small business game. For many, the answer has been a compromise between owning a business and retaining the security of working for a large company: Franchising.

New franchises pop up every day. The law of averages dictates that some of them will fail. Also some franchises may not match the prospective buyer's style or skills. Therefore, a responsibility of a book like this is to help you over some of the rough spots.

This book provides you with a road map when you look for your own franchise operation. Of course this book is not all you need when you hunt for the perfect franchise, but it should help you select the franchise that's right for you.

As you search for your franchise, you'll begin to understand that finding the right one involves a great deal of effort. You have to learn to look ahead and to resist the hard sells and fast pitches. The business you set up will succeed only because of your hard work and intelligent planning.

The primary point this book stresses is that finding the

right franchise is a job in itself. It should be treated the same as if you were hunting for a position in a company—with the difference that before you could go to work, you would have to invest most of your savings in that company.

This book also stresses that you cannot "go it alone." You need professional help—certainly a lawyer and probably an accountant. In the course of your hunt, some would-be advisors may claim that purchasing a franchise is a straightforward process that you can handle by yourself. Don't listen. In all probability you're looking for a franchise that will be a business you can manage, enjoy, and earn a decent living from for many years to come. Don't gamble your future by not getting the best advice possible right away. You may save some money initially, but 3, 5, even 10 years after you sign the franchising agreement, you may wish you had obtained professional counsel.

As you proceed through this book, you'll read a few negative things about franchising. It's meant to forewarn you as you search for your franchise. Thousands of Americans are still making a very good living—and a few are getting rich—thanks to franchising. Hopefully you will too.

This book has three parts. Part I defines franchising and helps you determine if you really want to purchase a franchise. Part I also shows you how to find franchises, tells you what to look for and to watch out for, shows you how to find professional help, and discusses financing.

Part II deals with the business side of franchising—se ecting a site, hiring employees, managing employees, promoting your business, and doing the basic bookkeeping.

Part III includes several checklists and provides a list of some existing franchise operations, including descriptions and start-up costs.

Part I

Finding Your Franchise

Chapter 1

Franchising – What to Expect

Types of Franchise / Types of Businesses Being Franchised / Franchising Opportunities Today / When Is a Franchise Not a Franchise?

IF YOU'VE PICKED UP this book, you probably have an urge to run your own business—for whatever reason—and you think a franchise might satisfy that urge. But do you understand what franchising is? Let's discuss right off some of the things you need to know about franchising.

First of all, a franchise is an excellent way to own your own business without all the headaches associated with starting a business by yourself. This is the big lure for many people. The franchisor often has had several years of hard-fought experience in the business and knows from trial and error what works and what doesn't. Usually your entire plan of action will be laid out for you by the franchisor. The only thing you have to worry about is following instructions, maintaining accurate records, and keeping the royalty checks in the mail.

Second, a franchise provides an opportunity. But remember, there are good opportunities and not so good ones. Often what works for one person, doesn't for another. A retired phys ed teacher might have a much better chance of succeeding with a health club than with a real estate agency. Furthermore, you get out of a franchise what you put into it. A franchise can give you a good chance to succeed, but you must be aware from the first that it involves a sizable risk.

Basically, franchising is a sort of symbiosis. An owner, who is known as the *franchisor*, licenses an independent businessperson, known as the *franchisee*, to sell the owner's product or service in a particular location. The franchisee generally pays a fee for this privilege, plus a royalty on gross sales. The term *franchise* can mean two things: the franchisee's right to sell a certain product or service, and the place of business where the franchisee exercises that right.

It is to the advantage of each party to have the business—the franchise—succeed. Obviously, the more the franchisee sells, the more he or she earns. The same is true for the franchisor; if the franchisee's sales continue to increase, the franchisor's royalty checks will snowball. If the franchisor can set up several successful franchises, he or she will earn a substantial amount of money.

This mutual relationship is what makes franchising so attractive to both franchisors and franchisees. There is a strong sense of interdependence. With a good franchise, the parent company tries very hard to help the franchisee succeed. Many franchisors have highly trained, thoroughly experienced staffs that provide training and advice. Also, with a good franchisor this help doesn't disappear after the initial training period.

The franchisor isn't just being kind to you; he or she wants to make sure that the franchise itself doesn't suffer. It's bad for the franchisor's business reputation when franchises fail.

The advantages for the franchisee include not having to worry about advertising, trademarks, design of the premises, sources of supplies, and, in general, the actual setting up of shop. A good franchise organization provides a wealth of information on all these subjects. In addition, many franchisors show you the ropes for almost every aspect of the business. And although relatively few offer financing these days, they can show you ways of obtaining loans and even help you obtain loans.

Types of Franchises

Three main types of franchising systems are available. They are all covered by the broad definition of franchising, but they function differently. One type includes the manufacturers that use franchises as a way to distribute their products such as the automobile companies and their dealerships. Other franchise companies sell products at wholesale to franchises that then retail those products. Finally there is the franchise system that is most common today, the franchisors who offer a name, an image, and a standardized method of doing business, such as McDonald's, Kentucky Fried Chicken, Holiday Inn, Gallery of Homes, and hundreds of others.

Many franchises offer services rather than products. Personnel agencies, real estate agencies, income tax experts—such franchises sell experience, established names, trademarks, and methods of doing business. In some cases, as in real estate agencies, the franchisee actually owns his or her own agency before applying to become a franchisee. The attraction of these businesses is their national advertising and national referral services.

Franchising has many wrinkles. In addition to operating franchises, in which you the businessperson runs the operation, a person can become licensed to do business on a larger scale as a licensed regional franchisor. A person in such a position is still a type of franchisee but can grant franchises in a particular area for the parent company. The regional franchisor's job is to develop franchises in a specified part of the country.

In this book I concentrate on the operating franchisee—a person searching for a small business to run on his or her own. After becoming successful, these individual franchisees may then purchase other franchises and become operators on a large scale. But this book is primarily concerned with the person looking for his or her first franchise.

Types of Businesses Being Franchised

Franchising involves many types of businesses. Besides the auto dealerships and fast-food franchises we're all familiar with, franchising also extends to such business areas as equipment rental, campgrounds, business services, travel agencies, personnel agencies, hotels, health spas, food shops, and dozens of others. (Part III includes a list of businesses, taken from a comprehensive government publication describing franchises across the country.)

Even more interesting, there is a great range of possible new areas being considered for franchised concerns. The data processing industry has already made a few franchising forays with the new computer stores that market small computers. That industry will probably go great guns in the future.

According to Joel D. Gingiss, president of the International Franchise Association, in a speech he made in September, 1980, there are many potential business arenas for franchising: electronics, education, and professional services are just a few. To Gingiss, franchising makes a great deal of sense for many businesses, because it provides a well-proved method of allowing people to step right into a business setting without the normal hassles associated with starting private concerns.

Both doctors and lawyers are among the possibilities Gingiss sees for franchising in the future. It might make a lot of sense for these busy professionals to become part of a franchise system that can take many of the day-to-day business and management problems off their hands. This would make expecially good sense for the new MD or lawyer just setting up shop. They face enormous start up costs and, beyond their professional expertise, usually don't have much experience in practical affairs. Besides, taboos about advertising by doctors and lawyers are beginning to tumble. A franchise—either local or national—could produce far more effective advertising than most individual practices could afford.

Indeed, some franchises have already started up in the health and legal fields. The only difficulty for you as a prospective franchisee is that unless you're only looking for an investment and don't plan to run the shop, you need a professional background for such franchises.

Medical and legal professionals, however, aren't the only people who may benefit by the franchise system in the future. Carpenters, plumbers, electricians, and other crafts-persons may find it profitable to band together under the banner of a well-known franchise operation. In fact, with proper backing and support, almost any product or service could be franchised.

Franchising Opportunities Today

There are certainly plenty of opportunities out there right now. Interesting new franchises range from maid services and burglar alarm businesses to delivery services and home computer stores. As you well know, however, buying any franchise is something of a gamble.

Say you read about a new franchise and send away for some information about it. This franchise has no national advertising, no long list of present franchisees you can talk to, no real record. Only plenty of promises. You can certainly buy a franchise from an outfit like this for much less money than you would pay for an established franchise such as a Holiday Inn or a Kentucky Fried Chicken. For those of you with limited budgets, new franchises may offer the best possibilities. Established franchises—especially fast-food franchises—have steadily increased in cost.

Do you want to take your chances on a fledgling company or make a larger investment in an established business that is more predictable in terms of how much income you can make right away? Obviously it is up to you. As you learn from this book, much of your success in finding a good franchise depends upon the amount of research you do. There are ways to find out facts about any franchise. Your research will, hopefully, reveal either that everything is on the up-and-up or that it is a bad bet. Your research won't provide you with a crystal ball, but with it you will be better armed against the vagaries of fortune.

When Is a Franchise Not a Franchise?

It is important to be aware that some business opportunities look like franchises but aren't. Some are perfectly legitimate, others are frauds.

One example of a business that appears to be a franchise but isn't is the kind that sells an identifiable, national product but sells it outright, demands no royalty fee, but also does not guarantee any territorial integrity to the purchaser either. This kind includes a well-known fitness equipment manufacturer. This company sells the equipment, and if the buyer meets certain standards set by the manufacturer, the buyer can use the name of the equipment in its own business name. The relationship ends there—except for the resupplying of equipment. This company has no interest in collecting any money beyond the price of its equipment. Once the buyers have bought the machines, they are free to do with them what they like. And, as actually has happened, competitors can open up an identical shop right across the street.

This particular company doesn't pretend to be a franchise: far from it; everything is fully explained at the start, and the business is cash on the line. This example points out, however, how important it is for you to know exactly what you are purchasing before you sign any contract. If you expect to receive a specific territory for your sales, it had better be spelled out in the agreement, in black and white.

Another business that looks a little like a franchise is the distributor who grants exclusive selling rights within a territory. This is not a franchise, because the parent company does not provide any help or guidance. It merely grants an authorized dealership and doesn't exercise any control. Of course there is nothing wrong with this type of business; it's often quite successful. It just isn't a franchise and doesn't offer the same benefits to the novice businessperson.

Another business that at first appears to be a franchise, but is vastly different from the franchising system, is the pyramid scheme. Illegal in many states, pyramid businesses depend on selling territories and dealerships to other investors. The original investors—those at the top of the pyramid—make a great deal of money exploiting the gullibility of others by selling them dealerships. In turn, these people sell still more pieces of dealerships to others. In the end, since many of these companies offer, at best, shoddy products, provide very spotty supply, and have too many dealers, the whole thing collapses of its own weight.

How do you tell if an operation is a pyramid? Often, you find yourself at the wrong end of a very hard sell. The glad handers sponsoring you tell you about the many successful operators and confide in hushed tones that so and so had over a million in sales. They may well have had a million in sales—but the money probably came from people who bought dealerships from them. The product probably also has a flashy or impressive name.

Perhaps you'll be asked to attend a gathering or convention, meet the successful salespeople in person, and see a film with some star touting the magnificence of the product. (These "stars" are well paid for these performances. The one I personally saw was a well-known song-and-dance man who hasn't worked on television in several years.) Then the talk gets around to how you can make really big money. One housewares product business carefully explains how to sell as many operations as possible to local housewives who would want to make some extra money. The actual product itself is rarely mentioned and the methods of distribution never are touched on. Nor is there any mention of advertising that would help this product achieve any acceptance in a highly competitive market.

In general, it is high-pressure salesmanship. But the crucial point is what the business really offers. If they offer you a once-in-a-lifetime chance to get rich by selling others on a product that you never heard of before, never saw in use, and that appears to you to have little chance of succeeding, you've either got a pyramid—or a sphinx.

I stress this point throughout this book: you must *thoroughly* understand the nature of the franchise you are about to purchase. This is vital. Sign no papers and certainly pay no money until you are totally secure with all arrangements and have had all your questions answered. This can't be stated too frequently. Your only real protection is the firm understanding of just what you're getting yourself into. It doesn't stop with knowing the business; you should know yourself and your limits. That is the topic of the next chapter.

Chapter 2

Is Franchising for You?

Take a Long, Hard Look at Franchising / Matching Yourself with a Franchise

Now that you know what a franchise is, you should ask yourself whether you're the type of person who is likely to enjoy operating a franchise, for you're far more likely to succeed at franchising if you enjoy what you're doing.

The brief quiz on page 22 can help you form a clearer idea about your suitability to run a small business.

If most of your choices on the quiz are in the right-hand column, you may be better off not attempting to run your own franchise. You'd probably make more money by investing in blue chip stocks. The items on the right describe a person who has little aptitude for an entrepreneurial style of operation. Such persons are likely to be more comfortable in a large organization than in a small business of their own.

On the other hand, if most of your choices are in the left-hand column, franchising may present you with some unique problems. You might be the sort of person who prefers to do things your own way. But in franchising, many things must be done the way the franchisors want them done. Clearly, however, the traits most useful in franchising are those in the left-hand column.

This quiz was developed for people who want to run their own small business. Franchising, though, is a little less implacable than operating a small business on your own, for you're not the only one looking out for your business's interests. Thus, people who chose a smattering of items in the quiz's middle column or even the right-hand column can most likely work well in franchising.

The quiz also implies that you have to be in the right shape physically as well as mentally. You may feel you are well able to take on the rigors of operating a franchise, but if you have physical limitations, you must pay attention to them when you select a business, especially if you are retired or disabled. Unless you have the proper help, some franchises are likely to put a substantial strain on your physical stamina. You might find it difficult to run a small fast-food restaurant on your own or with minimal help. Chances are you would have to be on your feet all day and have to do heavy lifting as well. And the hours are extremely long. The same might be true of franchises that involve a sizable inventory: constant lifting and shifting of merchandise can present a big problem to some people.

Take a Long, Hard Look at Franchising

Some aspects of franchising might strike you as advantages or disadvantages, turn-offs or turn-ons, depending on your own personality and how well you understand the actual workings of a franchise.

Owning a franchise is different from owning another small business to the extent that you have very little say in many aspects of the way the business is run. Many franchisors are very strict in their approach to business, as well they should be, for they have a large stake in how the public views their business. They often prefer uniformity in their franchises, since that permits greater control. But they usually base their style of operating on their extensive experience, which has shown them what works and what doesn't.

Most franchises offer standard products and services that

the franchisee can't change. There is a good reason for this standardized approach. It lends itself to quality control and provides customers with a product or service they don't have to guess about. If you walk into a McDonald's in Dallas, you get the same Big Mac that a McDonald's offers in London. This approach also makes it much easier to take advantage of advertising on both a local and national level. Just imagine if everyone who bought a franchise could do as they please. At one franchise the burger menu might be spiced up with souvlaki. Another owner of the same sort of franchise might decide that sushi would enliven his menu. Pretty soon what once was an identifiable burger chain would disintegrate into a mass of restaurants each doing its own thing. Thus the standardization works not just for the franchisor's benefit, but yours as well.

Franchisors do experiment, though. Fast-food chains are beginning to enlarge their menus with specialty sandwiches, desserts, and other entrees. These businesses often test new products in a few select locations, and if the products are well received the franchisor makes them available to franchises throughout the country, after launching a major national advertising campaign to create a demand for the new products. The essential fact, though, is that you yourself won't be free to experiment. You usually have to follow the rules and run the business the way the franchisor thinks best.

Franchising involves risks. Franchising has had its ups and downs. Everyone knows about the success of McDonald's, but you should also be aware that for every successful franchise several other companies have folded or, at best, barely kept their heads above water. In the golden days of franchising, it was possible to purchase a business for peanuts and watch it turn into a Burger King or a Kentucky Fried Chicken. Those days are, if not over, much more restricted.

Franchising isn't a life for passive people. Just because

you're backed by a major concern doesn't mean that they do all the work for you. And just because your franchise may have slick national advertising, that doesn't mean that all you have to do is sit back and watch the money roll in. You must remember that franchising is a way to own your own business, and it takes as much effort to run that franchised outlet as it would to run a business you started from scratch.

A few people use a franchise chiefly as an investment and hire a staff to run their business. But most people can't afford to hire high-priced managers. They have to do the managing themselves, getting their hands dirty and working hard. Fast-food franchises, for example, often demand a lot of dedication from their owners. A restaurant manager may have to put in 60 hours or more each week, staying open 7 days a week and even on holidays. Most fast-food franchise owners have a staff, but even so, as manager, he or she is expected to be at the establishment most of the time—ready, in a pinch, to take over any of the jobs.

Now, after being completely honest with yourself, if you still feel that owning your own franchise is the life for you, then plunge ahead. However, be forewarned. Finding the right franchise for you is a job in itself. It shouldn't be approached lightly. You're gambling on your future, and you want to be absolutely sure that the decision you make is the best one. This means doing a great deal of research, asking hard questions, and being tough-minded. You can't fall for sweet sales talks or be hypnotized by promised riches. Reality often comes too soon after you sign the franchise agreement. You have to know right up front what you're going to get. The only surprise you want from your business is that your earnings were even higher than you anticipated.

Matching Yourself with a Franchise

Part of knowing yourself means understanding what particular franchise would be best for you. As Part III shows, there are hundreds of businesses to choose from. You must be convinced that the one you choose is right for you.

What is your situation now? Are you stuck in a regular nine-to-five job and want out? Are you retired or about to retire and want a new business? Are you a woman who wants to reenter the business world? Are you a member of a minority with a great deal of drive but very little money?

Some of you have a better chance in certain franchises than others. And some of you are eligible for a great deal of help. The federal government has established a Minority Business Development Agency whose purpose is to help set up new minority enterprises and to help existing minority enterprises expand. For more information, you can write:

Deputy Director for Program Resources
Minority Business Development Agency
U.S. Department of Commerce
Washington DC 20230
Telephone: 202–337–2025

The *Franchise Opportunities Handbook*, put out by the federal government, also has a list of regional resource centers.

Another source of help for everyone is the Small Business Administration (SBS). In addition to a variety of useful publications, the SBA also is a major source of loans for small businesses. This is covered more fully in Chapter 7. Regional offices of the SBA are listed in Chapter 6.

Remember, just about the most important element to consider when you look for a franchise is whether you will enjoy it. All the money in the world won't help if you detest your job. So pick a franchise that you'll want to work at.

Mismatch—Misfortune

Tom, a retired history professor, was seduced by the prospect of a good income when he purchased an auto parts franchise. It was a good, solid business. Tom, an intelligent man, did everything right. He checked other franchisees, brought in an accountant and lawyer, contacted the local Better Business Bureau, and compared the business with the competition. He got a very good deal. Yet Tom was out of business within a year. The primary reason was that Tom and his business really didn't match. The auto parts company salesman recognized that Tom was a little out of place, but Tom saw only the profits. He felt that the money coming in would offset any disadvantages of running an operation he didn't really like. But a few weeks after the excitement of owning his own business wore off, Tom was left with the reality of spark plugs, mufflers, and shock absorbers. He had to eat, breathe, and live auto parts 6 days a week. In fairness, he ran a smooth operation, but he couldn't really adapt— either to the clientele or the daily grind.

Tom was lucky; he was dealing with a solid, respectable company that was glad to buy back his business and mark him off as one of the few bad bets that slipped through their screening process. But Tom's mistake illustrates an important point. You are, in most cases, going to eat, breathe, and live your business for 60 hours a week or more. So you had better select a business that can challenge you and can hold your interest in addition to making you a tidy profit.

Solid Future Built on Present Skills

Sue, also a teacher, was more successful than Tom. She not only wanted out of a dead-end teaching job, she wanted to run her own business and make a lot of money. So she set out looking for a business that would enable her to do what she liked best—working with and helping people. After carefully looking through list after list of types of businesses, Sue settled on a personnel agency. The one she selected offered an excellent training program and good managerial help. She was enthusiastic about running her own business, and she knew she could use the skills she had developed in teaching. And she was correct in her choice. She maintained her high level of enthusiasm and enjoyed the challenge of working hard to make a go of her business. In short, Sue liked what she did and that made all the difference in the world.

Franchising offers you plenty of choices. Certainly there are other considerations—financial for one—but don't select a business just on the basis of the money you might make. To start, read through the list of franchises provided in Part III. Then check other sources for franchises, particularly the *Franchising Opportunities Handbook*.

Take some time to compare several businesses. If you haven't had any experience in the area you're considering, try to imagine how you'd feel working on the job. Try to imagine yourself working at the same business in another 5 years. Will it still feel good?

Rating Scale for Personal Traits Important to a Business Proprietor

Instructions. After each question place a check mark on the line at the point closest to your answer. The check mark need not be placed directly over one of the suggested answers because your rating may lie somewhere between two answers. Be honest with yourself.

Are you a self-starter?

I do things my own way. Nobody needs to tell me to get going.	If someone gets me started, I keep going all right.	Easy does it. I don't put myself out until I have to.

How do you feel about other people?

I like people. I can get along with just about anybody.	I have plenty of friends. I don't need anyone else.	Most people bug me.

Can you lead others?

I can get most people to go along without much difficulty.	I can get people to do things if I drive them.	I let someone else get things moving.

Can you take responsibility?

I like to take charge of and see things through.	I'll take over if I have to, but I'd rather let someone else be responsible.	There's always some eager beaver around wanting to show off. I say let him.

How good an organizer are you?

I like to have a plan before I start. I'm usually the one to get things lined up.	I do all right unless things get too goofed up. Then I cop out.	I just take things as they come.

How good a worker are you?

I can keep going as long as necessary. I don't mind working hard.	I'll work hard for a while, but when I've had enough, that's it!	I can't see that hard work gets you anywhere.

Can you make decisions?

I can make up my mind in a hurry if necessary, and my decision is usually o.k.	I can if I have plenty of time. If I have to make up my mind fast, I usually regret it.	I don't like to be the one who decides things. I'd probably blow it.

Can people trust what you say?

They sure can. I don't say things I don't mean.	I try to be on the level, but sometimes I just say what's easiest.	What's the sweat if the other fellow doesn't know the difference?

Can you stick with it?

If I make up my mind to do something, I don't let anything stop me.	I usually finish what I start.	If a job doesn't go right, I turn off. Why beat your brains out?

How good is your health?

I never run down.	I have enough energy for most things I want to do.	I run out of juice sooner than most of my friends seem to.

Chapter 3

Finding the Right Franchise

Questioning Franchise Operators

THERE ARE MANY things for you to consider when searching for your franchise. At this point, you should be quite confident that you are the type of person who could succeed with a franchise. And you also know something about the type of business you're interested in. The next part is critical—matching your criteria to a specific franchise.

How do you actually go about finding your franchise? It's quite easy. In addition to the list of franchised businesses in the back of this book, several publications—newspapers and magazines—offer franchising opportunities. The *New York Times*, the *Wall Street Journal*, and *Money Magazine* are good sources. If you rummage around in the back of magazines like *Popular Mechanics* and *Popular Science*, you'll find other advertisements for franchises.

There are also conventions, franchise brokers (business-people who handle the sales of franchises), trade shows, and franchise associations where you can obtain information. (You can find their addresses in Chapter 6.) There are literally hundreds of ways to obtain information.

Once you have a list of names and the basic facts as published, you've reached the starting point. The hard part is the careful sorting of the reams of material that you will obtain from the companies you decide to contact. And you should contact as many as you can to get a fair sampling of what's available. This is not a process to be rushed. You should leave no stone unturned—because any hazy or vague statements that you shrug off in the thrill of obtaining your own business could come back to haunt you.

Once you've written away for material, you should use a checklist like the following one for comparing the businesses. This will be the first rough pass, a way of narrowing down your choices. Carefully check prospective franchises to see whether they appear likely to:

- Provide adequate profits
- Have a strong future
- Provide high-quality products or services
- Offer you adequate training
- Provide you with adequate support
- Have a clean record
- Spell out all terms and conditions in the contract—to your satisfaction

At this stage you may want to contact directly a few franchises that appear the most attractive to you. By now you'll have obtained a copy of their disclosure statement (the next chapter describes the disclosure statement in detail), and you'll have a rough idea of the capital you have to come up with in order to purchase the franchise and keep it in operation.

Throughout this process you'll be corresponding and meeting with various people representing the franchise. Get to know them, since they are your line to the heart of the business. Question them closely about the franchise operation. And be sure to ask all the hard questions. Take your checklist along and fill it with the information you obtain from these people. Then take another checklist and fill it with information you have found on your own. Do they match? If not, it might be a good idea to go back and ask why there are discrepancies.

After you hear from the franchise representatives, how do you check on the franchise? There are several sources. You first should see if they have had any previous complaints lodged against them. Check the record of the business through the Better Business Bureau. Another source might be Dun and Bradstreet. The disclosure statement will tell you if the franchise has been sued. If they have been sued, then the big question is, what was the result?

Don't stop with the company. Try to discover what kind of backgrounds the chief executive officers have. Are the executives involved with other franchises, or have they ever been involved with franchises that went out of business? If so, why did the businesses fold? If all this seems a little obtrusive, just remember that if the franchisors you're investigating are good, they will be even more carefully checking into your background.

Questioning Franchise Operators

Probably the most important source of information available to you will be those businesspersons who have taken the plunge before you. You'll probably have received a selected list of some of the business's franchisees from the franchisor. Talk to them. Ask them as many questions as possible about the operation. Are they satisfied? If they had it to do over again, would they choose the same franchise? Did the company's forecast of the amount of money they would need turn out to be accurate? How about their expenses—did they jibe with company predictions?

These people are extremely important to you. They've been there. Ask them about their experiences and try to put yourself in their places. And don't stop at one or two. See between five and ten. And don't just see the franchisees the franchisor directs you to. Check around and see if there are any others in your area who aren't on the list. If not, go to the library and search for out-of-town or even out-of-state franchisees and give them a call. Their information may be worth the price of a long-distance conversation.

Unsettling Discoveries

Don was certainly glad he had uncovered a few additional franchisees not mentioned by the company. After some long talks, Don discovered that a few of these franchisees were very unhappy. They had not participated in a supposedly voluntary company program, and in retaliation the company turned the screws on. One of the franchisees was stubborn and was in the process of bringing a lawsuit against the company.

These findings by themselves didn't cause Don to decide against this particular franchise. But in conjunction with other things he learned, they proved to be deciding factors. In the end, Don selected another franchise.

I can't stress too much how important these people can be to you. The franchiser you talk to is standing where you might be standing in a few years. Take a long hard look. Is that where you want to be? After you've visited a few of these franchisees, analyze what you've discovered. Is there a large disparity between the most successful and the least successful franchisees you've met? If there is, dig a little deeper into why one was more—or less—successful than another. This isn't necessarily a bad sign. If there are very successful franchisees and it is apparent why they are more successful—better management, better location, and so on—there's no reason you can't succeed too.

But talk to them at length. One way or another, they'll give you a great deal of information. If they've been successful, they'll be proud to tell you why. If they haven't been successful, they'll give you some insight into the way the franchise operates when the chips are down.

By now you have eliminated for one reason or another all but those franchises that appear to have the most potential. You should now go back over the material the franchisors have given you and recheck it. Does everything fit into place? Are there any rough edges? Have the franchise people you have dealt with been helpful and encouraging, or have they been high pressure and full of hazy promises that can't be easily substantiated?

Chapter 4

The Disclosure Statement and the Contract

The Franchise Contract

AT SOME POINT in your dealings with the franchisor you must obtain a disclosure statement, which is also called a prospectus. The law requires franchisors to make available such a statement. However, the franchisor is not obligated to provide you with a prospectus until 10 days before the signing of the contract. You will need much more time than that to check the statements and compare them with other offerings. Therefore make sure that you request a disclosure statement right up front in your dealings with any company.

The disclosure statement is supposed to help you understand the franchise you are considering. Some statements are better written and more comprehensive than others, but all are required to contain the following information (according to the *Franchising Opportunities Handbook* of the United States Department of Commerce):

1. Identification of the franchisor and its affiliates and their business experience
2. The business experience of each of the franchisor's officers, directors, and management personnel responsible for franchise services, training, and other aspects of the franchise programs

3. The lawsuits in which the franchisor and its officers, directors, and management personnel have been involved

4. Any previous bankruptcies in which the franchisor and its officers, directors, and management personnel have been involved

5. The initial franchise fee and other initial payments that are required to obtain the franchise

6. The continuing payments that franchisees are required to make after the franchise opens

7. Any restrictions on the quality of goods and services used in the franchise and where they may be purchased, including restrictions requiring purchases from the franchisor or its affiliates

8. Any assistance available from the franchisor or its affiliates in financing the purchase of the franchise

9. Restrictions on the goods or services franchisees are permitted to sell

10. Any restrictions on the customers with whom franchisees may deal

11. Any territorial protection that will be granted to the franchisee

12. The conditions under which the franchise may be repurchased or refused renewal by the franchisor, transferred to a third party by the franchisee, and terminated or modified by either party

13. The training programs provided to franchisees

14. The involvement of any celebrities or public figures in the franchise

15. Any assistance in selecting a site for the franchise that will be provided by the franchisor

16. Statistical information about the present number of franchises; the number of franchises projected for the future; and the number of franchises terminated, the number the franchisor has decided not to renew, and the number repurchased in the past

17. The financial statement of the franchisor
18. The extent to which the franchisees must personally participate in the operation of the franchise
19. A complete statement of the basis for any earnings claims made to the franchisee, including the percentage of existing franchises that have actually achieved the results that are claimed
20. A list of the names and addresses of other franchises

The list appears pretty comprehensive, doesn't it? In reality, there are plenty of loopholes in it that can be taken advantage of by unscrupulous franchisors. The disclosure statement can be used by you as a resource in your search for a good franchise, and you should use it as such. But never accept a company's disclosure statement at face value.

Here's how the Federal Trade Commission views disclosure statements:

> To protect you, we've required your franchisor to give you this information. *We haven't checked it, and don't know if it's correct.* It should help you make up your mind. Study it carefully. While it includes some information about your contract, don't rely on it alone to understand your contract. Read all of your contract carefully. Buying a franchise is a complicated investment. Take your time to decide. If possible, show your contract and this information to an advisor, like a lawyer or accountant. If you find anything you think may be wrong or anything important that's been left out, you should let us know about it. It may be against the law.

This direct and strong statement should make clear the risks you'll be taking if you neglect to double-check all the details of the disclosure statement and don't read between the lines.

The Franchise Contract

The final step you take before signing over your money and your life is to study the proposed contract. This is not a matter for you to deal with alone. You need the counsel of a lawyer, preferably one well experienced in franchise negotiations. (See Chapter 6 on obtaining professional help.)

The contract will contain all the provisions that spell out your working agreement with the franchisor: how long the franchise is granted for, the rules governing renewal, the price, schedule of payments, royalties to be paid, penalties for late payments, and so on.

Everything should be clear to you. Don't leave anything to your imagination, and don't accept any verbal guarantees. Your lawyer, who should be experienced with franchises, is your best guide here. But you will have to work closely with him or her. If, over the course of your investigation, you have any question at all about the franchise, ask it. If you feel uneasy about any clause, try to have it changed to your satisfaction.

Remember, virtually anything can be negotiated. Even though the franchisor hands you a beautifully printed contract that is ripe for signing, hold off. Hand the contract to your lawyer for his or her perusal. You'll be surprised at the lack of regard your lawyer has for the printed page. Stipulations, rules, transferals—all are subject to negotiation. Your lawyer's chief concern should be that you get as fair a deal as possible.

Of course, the franchisor will have a legal staff too, and probably a fair amount of experience in negotiation. The franchisor will also know that if you've been doing your homework, you'll know that the contracts aren't the same for everyone in the organization.

If your lawyer can't make any headway against changing what he or she considers a bad provision, you have to make a decision about whether or not to sign the contract. Follow your lawyer's advice in this. The next chapter deals, in part, with the murky contract clauses that should give you pause.

Chapter 5

Pitfalls

*The New Franchise / The Dishonest Franchisor /
Hazy Contracts / Pressure from the Franchisor /
Money Requirements / Competition / The Future
of Your Franchise / Legal Rights and a Code of
Ethics*

AT ONE POINT in the mid-sixties there were so many con
artists operating that the name franchising began to suffer.
Too many schemes and stings were fleecing unsuspecting
people of their investments. These con artists were successful because franchising was thriving. Some people actually
did make a bundle out of a small investment, and that made
others ripe for high-pressure, pie-in-the-sky offerings.

Those days have passed, and today the consumer has
substantially more governmental protection. But again, that
protection if far from proof against swindlers—and it is even
less proof against concerns that are honest but poorly run.

The New Franchise

How do you check the statements of a brand-new franchise,
a business that has been in operation for a year or less? If you
check with the few franchisecs who have already purchased
their franchise, in all probability you'll get glowing statements from enthusiastic owners—owners who haven't had
time yet to become disillusioned.

Although new franchises present a few problems, you'd
be smart to check as deeply as possible into the backgrounds
of the directors and managers of the franchise company. If

you discover that they have had several previous concerns that have been less than successful, you certainly should be a bit skeptical about the potential of the present venture.

Compare the new franchisor's estimations of earnings and costs with those of similar concerns that have been in business several years. Are they in line or are they wildly disparate? Remember, you're not getting something for nothing. Question claims over and over again. Find out how the franchisors arrived at their estimates. Just because there are lists of numbers on a page doesn't mean those figures can be taken as gospel.

A new franchise is an enormous gamble, but you may have another McDonald's on your hands. Take the extra few steps to do some hard thinking and research on your own. Perhaps the new franchise is in a business that hasn't been franchised before. Someone may have decided to franchise video game arcades. In your mind you can already hear the plink of quarters as happy video warriors shoot down outer space aliens with glee. These arcades have received a great deal of attention from the press in recent months, but do they have any future? At this stage no one knows for sure. Much depends upon the type of games developed in the coming years. Will they hold the attention of consumers? Will home video games affect the arcades as television did the motion picture theaters? How about town ordinances: will they restrict arcades from the most lucrative locations? Will your arcade attract an unsavory element that eventually puts you out of business?

The Dishonest Franchisor

There are still out-and-out frauds, but if you are careful, they can be easily weeded out—just by following the steps provided by the checklist in Chapter 8. If you do stumble on a franchisor who is working against the law, report him or her to the program advisor for the Franchise and Business

Opportunities Program, which is administered by the Federal Trade Commission. The government can levy a fine of up to $10,000 for every violation of federal laws.

If you follow through on investigating the operation, it should be apparent whether the franchise is violating any agreements or is publishing incorrect figures. The other franchisees can help you here, as well as your lawyer and accountant. If the franchisees are getting a raw deal, they'll let you know in a hurry. The Small Business Administration will have a list of complaints too. The only difficulty is when the franchise is brand new, and the protection in that case has already been discussed.

Hazy Contracts

A bigger threat to you are hazy contracts. You'll probably sign a contract for ten years, although some contracts are for five or twenty years. What will you have after the ten years is up? Some franchisees who did not have their contracts renewed watched their carefully nurtured businesses go right down the tubes when they were forced to sell them back to the franchisor. See what protection you have against this.

Termination clauses can be murky. Make sure the franchise contract spells out in detail the circumstances under which your contract can be canceled. In most cases, franchise agreements can be terminated by the franchisor only when good cause is shown, such as when, for example, the franchisee has done something to harm the franchise's image—a burger restaurant owner introduces porkburgers. Or the contract may be canceled because the franchisee is in arrears with royalty payments. This is a sore point, because some franchisors who want a franchisee out may use a slightly late payment as an excuse.

Extraordinary as it may sound, some franchisees can lose their businesses because they are too successful. This may be due to a great deal of greed on the franchisor's part. Or the franchisor may decide that he wants to change his franchised operation into a chain store business in which the managers of the outlets are all employees of a company, rather than independent business operators.

In any event, you can quickly lose your business unless you have closely investigated all of the clauses in your contract. If you take a franchisor to court on the grounds that he or she is unfairly terminating your contract, you may discover that the judge will say that you had ample opportunity to read the contract before you signed it. The lesson here is that you need experienced counsel before signing any contract.

Pressure from the Franchisor

Another problem is the franchisor who exerts a little under-the-table pressure to keep the franchisees in line. One fast-food company has a reputation for subtly maintaining order. Its special promotions are supposedly voluntary, but if the franchisees don't go along with the promotion, they may find that their deliveries are late. This franchisor also has a reputation of buying out successful franchises.

How do you protect yourself against this type of headache? Simple. Do your research. Check with as many current franchisees as possible. If you get the slightest whiff that everything is not as it appears, a warning light should go off in your head. At that point, dig deeper. The disclosure statement should give the number of stores that have closed for any reason. This figure may have been whitewashed, but if the number seems inordinately high, again you should take pause. Also, don't forget to find out about past and pending law suits—and check with the Better Business Bureau. When you've done all this and had your questions answered to your satisfaction, you should be in a position to make a reasonable choice.

Another form of coercion sometimes occurs in the arrangements that franchisors set up for the purchase of supplies by their franchises. Many franchisors can provide supplies at a reduced rate to their many franchisees because of bulk buying procedures. However, in certain instances franchisees who have done some research in buying have discovered that they can get the same supplies for less money from other suppliers. In some cases, the franchisees have a point. Certain franchises have made a good deal of money by forcing their franchisees to purchase all materials from them at a hefty price. Yet, the franchisors also have a good point when they insist that buying cut-rate from other suppliers might reduce the ultimate quality of the products and hurt the image of the franchise.

Who is right? There have been several lawsuits on this issue, and it is now illegal in many areas to force franchisees to buy supplies only from the franchisor. The best way for you to deal with the subject is to do your research before you sign any papers. If you discover that buying supplies is a sore point with other franchisees in the business you are interested in, you may want to look elsewhere.

Money Requirements

Many of the people who get burned today are those with stars in their eyes, the same kind of people who would buy Arizona wasteland without checking the property first. When you're promised the moon, watch out for the craters.

One important number to question is the total start-up fee. If you scrape up just enough capital to cover what the franchisor claims you need, you may be out on a very insecure limb. You have to realize that even the best intentioned franchisors can only estimate expenses. And some franchisors might think nothing of estimating on the low side. The end result is that you may be forced into a position in which you just can't get your head above water.

Underestimates Can Hurt

John took his franchisor at face value when the franchisor swore he only needed $80,000 to start his fast-food franchise. It soon proved that the $80,000 figure was not correct. John needed more than $100,000 to start his business. The reasons for the discrepancy were that the franchisor's dollar figures didn't account for inflation, and John was setting up shop in a high-priced East coast location. John borrowed the extra money, but at a prohibitive interest rate. He saw his profits quickly eaten up by interest payments. The end result was that John had to get out of the business and sell his franchise at a loss.

The rule is, check and recheck all estimates of all costs that the franchisor gives you. Try to picture the unsuspected costs that may pop up. And, most important, try to give yourself a little breathing room. Don't overextend yourself in order to purchase a franchise. Pick one that you are sure that you can afford.

More on financing and financial planning will be covered in Chapter 9.

Competition

Discovering your competition is an important part of research in a prospective franchise. Competition takes many forms. You may find that the product your prospective franchise sells may be in direct competition with an overwhelming assortment of excellent products that have good support from their companies and are well promoted. You have to ask yourself whether you can you make a living selling in that sort of market. More on competition is presented in Chapter 9 on selecting your franchise's location.

The Future of Your Franchise

Try to think about the future. Have your prospective franchise operation's sales shown a steady deterioration over the past few years? Do you think this trend will continue? The business may well have reached the saturation point and can only steadily decline from now on.

Some franchises are based upon a single product or service. A change in public tastes or the introduction of a new product can have a terrible effect upon such a business. The dry cleaning business suffered when wash-and-wear fabrics were introduced. Diaper services virtually disappeared thanks to disposable diapers. Even discos are on the way out.

The warning here is to understand that there are risks involved in putting all your eggs in a single basket. Of course you can't predict the future, but you can certainly avoid those businesses that appear to be on their last legs. You also can stay away from fads—franchises that are brand new and offer something that has a great potential for failure—fast-food frog legs, to take an example from the Muppets.

Furthermore, it is impossible to predict all the trends, upswings, and downswings of the economy that can affect a business. This is also true of established franchises. How many people today are buying franchises that sell only large-sized American cars? Dictates of the economy can severely affect the most careful plans.

The point is that you have to be extremely careful when selecting any franchise—even one with a national name. Yet once you collect the material from your extensive research, you'll be armed with a substantial amount of facts that can tell you a great deal about your business. It's up to you to interpret that material.

Legal Rights and a Code of Ethics

Here are two lists that should help you when you investigate your prospective franchise. The first is a summary of your legal rights, and the second is the International Franchise Association's code of ethics.

Summary of Your Legal Rights. The Federal Trade Commission provides you with a fair amount of protection. Under the commission's rules you have these legal rights:

1. The right to receive a disclosure statement at your first personal meeting with a representative of the franchisor to discuss the purchase of a franchise; but in no event less than 10 business days before you sign a franchise or related agreement, or pay any money in connection with the purchase of a franchise.

2. The right to receive documentation stating the basis and assumptions for any earnings claims that are made at the time the claims are made; but in no event less than 10 days before you sign a franchise or related agreement, or pay any money in connection with the purchase of a franchise. If an earnings claim is made in advertising, you have the right to receive the required documentation at your first personal meeting with a representative of the franchisor.

3. The right to receive sample copies of the franchisor's standard franchise agreement and related agreements at the same time as you receive the disclosure statement, and the right to receive the final agreements you are to sign at least 5 business days before you sign them.

4. The right to receive any refunds promised by the franchisor, subject to any conditions or limitations on that right that have been disclosed by the franchisor.

5. The right not to be misled by oral or written representations made by the franchisor or its representatives that are inconsistent with the disclosures made in the disclosure statement.

These are your rights, but you must be aware of them at the outset. The government has no idea whether or not the material the franchisor sends you is accurate. It is up to you to find that out.

International Franchise Association's Code of Ethics. The legitimate franchise organizations, which far outnumber the bad operations, are determined to maintain the good reputation of franchising. The following is a code of ethics subscribed to by the International Franchise Association. See how your prospective franchisor matches with the code.

1. No member shall offer, sell, or promote the sale of any franchise, product, or service by means of any explicit or implied representation that is likely to have a tendency to deceive or mislead prospective purchasers of such franchise, product, or service.

2. No member shall imitate the trademark, trade name, corporate name, slogan, or other mark of identification of another business in any manner or form that would have the tendency or capacity to mislead or deceive.

3. The pyramid or chain distribution system is inimical to prospective investors and to the franchise system of distribution, and no member shall engage in any form of pyramid or chain distribution.

4. An advertisement, considered in its totality, shall be free from ambiguity and, in whatever form presented, must be considered in its entirety and as it would be read and understood by those to whom it is directed.

5. All advertisements shall comply, in letter and spirit, with all applicable rules, regulations, directives, guides, and laws promulgated by any governmental body or agency having jurisdiction.

6. An advertisement containing or making reference, directly or indirectly, to performance records, figures, or data respecting income or earnings of franchises shall be factual, and, if necessary to avoid deception, accurately qualified as to geographical area and time periods covered.

7. An advertisement containing information or making reference to the investment requirements of a franchise shall be as detailed as necessary to avoid being misleading in any way and shall be specific with respect as to whether the

stated amount(s) is a partial or the full cost of the franchise, the items paid for by the stated amount(s), financing requirements, and other costs.

8. Full and accurate written disclosure of all information considered material to the franchise relationship shall be given to prospective franchisees a reasonable time prior to the execution of any binding document, and members shall otherwise fully comply with federal and state laws requiring advance disclosure of information to prospective franchisees.

9. All matters to the franchise relationship shall be contained in one or more written agreements, which shall clearly set forth the terms of the relationship and the respective rights and obligations of the parties.

10. A franchisor shall select and accept only those franchisees who, upon reasonable investigation, appear to possess the basic skills, education, personal qualities, and financial resources adequate to perform and fulfill the needs and requirements of the franchise. There shall be no discrimination based on race, color, religion, national origin, or sex.

11. The franchisor shall encourage and/or provide training designed to help franchisees improve their abilities to conduct their franchises.

12. A franchisor shall provide reasonable guidance and supervision over the business activities of franchisees for the purpose of safeguarding the public interest and of maintaining the integrity of the entire franchise system for the benefit of all parties having an interest in it.

13. Fairness shall characterize all dealings between a franchisor and its franchisees. To the extent reasonably appropriate under the circumstances, a franchisor shall give notice to its franchisee of any contractual breach and grant reasonable time to remedy default.

14. A franchisor should be conveniently accessible and responsive to communications from franchisees, and provide a mechanism by which ideas may be exchanged and

areas of concern discussed for the purpose of improving mutual understanding and reaffirming mutuality of interest.

15. A franchisor shall make every effort to resolve complaints, grievances, and disputes with its franchisees with good faith and good will through fair and reasonable direct communication and negotiation. Failing this, consideration should be given to mediation or arbitration.

Chapter 6

Getting Professional Help

*Accountants and Lawyers / The Small Business
Administration / Franchising Organizations*

FINDING THE RIGHT FRANCHISE is a complicated business—
even a potentially dangerous task—unless you get some
good professional help. Going it alone is like picking your
way through an enemy minefield. Even in dealing with
solid, well-established franchises, things can go wrong.
There are too many hidden or hazy clauses that look just fine
in the flush of buying, but might not look so good months or
years down the road. Then you might discover the true
meaning of the fine print that you thought was just meaning-
less legalese.

After you purchase your franchise, there are still other
professionals you should stay in touch with. These are people who can give you advice and provide you with the extra
level of security in business affairs.

Accountants and Lawyers

There are two professionals you need in the franchise investigation stage—an accountant and a lawyer. It would be
especially wise if you picked professionals who have experience dealing specifically with franchises. Don't hire your
niece just out of law school or your uncle who is a retired
CPA. You need seasoned professionals primarily to check,

44

first, the financial statement and, second, the contract you sign.

What can these professionals tell you? First, the accountant can tell you if the figures you obtained through the disclosure statement make sense. A good accountant can spot inaccuracies or subtle jugglings. If an accountant is experienced in dealing with franchises, he or she will spot any discrepancies. The only way an accountant can be totally fooled is if the franchise company supplies figures for another concern. If that happens, you obviously have strong legal recourse.

The accountant also should be able to tell you whether or not the franchisor's projections are in line with reality. If they aren't, your accountant should be able to create a forecast of income and expenses. Take this forecast back to the franchisor and ask him or her why the two don't match.

The lawyer is even more vital. A sharp lawyer can read the proffered contract and explain step by step what the franchisor's obligations are and what yours are. He or she will be able to inform you about all the clauses in which you might lose your franchise. If these clauses are unacceptable to you, the lawyer will negotiate for better terms or advise you to look elsewhere if a favorable response can't be obtained.

Another reason you should obtain the services of a lawyer familiar with franchising is that he or she can counsel you on all the existing state and federal franchising laws. Certain taxation and insurance procedures must be followed. Hopefully, your franchisor provides all this information, but it is helpful to have a knowledgeable lawyer in your corner to act as both watchdog and backup.

How do you find these professionals? Don't just pick names out of the phone book. You want qualified, experienced people in your corner. After all, the franchisor probably has the best, so why shouldn't you? Indeed, you might spend more by having these professionals working for you, but you shouldn't quibble about a few dollars when your future is at stake.

One way to find both a good accountant and a good lawyer is through referals. Ask other franchisees or small business owners in your area who they used; see if they were satisfied with their legal counsel. If you have a personal lawyer, see if he or she can give you the name of an excellent business lawyer. Also, do some comparison shopping. Talk to a couple of lawyers or accountants to give yourself a choice.

Just before you go into business or even after you've opened shop, there are professionals you should be in touch with. You will need both your lawyer and accountant on a continuing basis: your accountant to prepare your taxes and your lawyer to keep you up to date on changes in local laws that may affect your business.

Other professionals include your bank officer, SBA employees, and the franchisor's staff. The bank officers are almost partners in your business if you've borrowed money from their bank. They know you, and they know their community. They may be in a position to more readily loan you more money if your business expands.

The Small Business Administration

The SBA is a marvelous source of information—most of it free.

The Small Business Administration aids those planning to enter business as well as to those in business. This assistance includes counseling and possible financial aid.

Counseling may be by SBA specialists or retired executives under the Service Corps of Retired Executives (SCORE) program, and could include various seminars or courses, or a combination of services including reference publications.

Financial assistance may take the form of loans or the participation in, or guaranty of, loans made by financial institutions. Such assistance can be given only to those eligible applicants who can't provide the money from their own resources and can't obtain it on reasonable terms from banks, franchisors, or other usual business sources.

The SBA financial support under its own legislation can provide up to $350,000 with the usual maximum maturity of 6 years for working capital and up to 10 years for fixtures and equipment. Under some circumstances, portions of a loan involving construction can qualify for longer terms up to 20 years. For those who qualify, loans made under Title IV of the Economic Opportunity Act can be up to $100,000 and the maturity can be up to 10 for working capital and 15 years for fixed assets.

A list follows of SBA field offices where more detailed information regarding the various services available can be obtained.

Regional Offices

Region 1: Connecticut, Maine, Massachusetts, New Hampshire, Rhode Island, Vermont
150 Causeway St., 10th Floor, Boston, MA 02203 (617) 223–2100.

Region 2: New Jersey, New York, Puerto Rico, Virgin Islands
26 Federal Plaza, Rm. 3930, New York, NY 10007 (212) 264–1468.

Region 3: Delaware, District of Columbia, Maryland, Pennsylvania, Virginia, West Virginia
231 St. Asaphs Road, Bala Cynwyd, PA 19004 (215) 597–3311.

Region 4: Alabama, Florida, Georgia, Kentucky, Mississippi, North Carolina, South Carolina, Tennessee
1401 Peachtree St., N.E., Rm. 441, Atlanta, GA 30309 (404) 526–0111

Region 5: Illinois, Indiana, Michigan, Minnesota, Ohio, Wisconsin
Federal Bldg., 219 South Dearborn St., Rm. 838, Chicago, IL 60604 (312) 353–4400

Region 6: Arkansas, Louisiana, New Mexico, Oklahoma, Texas
1720 Regal Row, Regal Park Office Bldg., Dallas, TX 75235 (214) 749–1011

Region 7: Iowa, Kansas, Missouri, Nebraska
911 Walnut St., 23rd Floor, Kansas City, MO 64106 (816) 374–7212

Region 8: Colorado, Montana, North Dakota, South Dakota, Utah, Wyoming
1405 Curtis St., Denver, CO 80202 (303) 327–0111

Region 9: Arizona, California, Hawaii, Nevada, Pacific Islands
Federal Bldg., 450 Golden Gate Ave., San Francisco, CA 94102 (415) 556–9000.

Region 10: Alaska, Idaho, Oregon, Washington
710 2nd Ave., 5th Floor, Dexter Horton Bldg., Seattle, WA 98104 (206) 442–4343

District Offices

Region 1

302 High St., Holyoke, MA 01040 (413) 536–8770

Federal Bldg., 40 Western Ave., Rm. 512, Augusta, ME 04330 (207) 622–6171

55 Pleasant St., Rm. 213, Concord, NH 03301 (603) 224–4041

One Financial Plaza, Hartford, CT 06103 (203) 244–3600

Federal Bldg., 87 State St., Rm. 210, Montpelier, VT 05602 (802) 229–0538

57 Eddy St., Rm. 710, Providence, RI 02903 (401) 528–4580

Region 2

Chardon and Bolivia Sts., Hato Rey, PR 00919 (809) 763–6363

970 Broad St., Rm. 1635, Newark, NJ 07102 (201) 645–2424

100 State Street, Room 601, Rochester, N.Y. 14614 (716) 263–6700

Federal Bldg., Rm. 1071, 100 South Clinton St., Syracuse, NY 13202 (315) 423–5383

111 West Huron St., Room 1311, Federal Bldg., Buffalo, NY 14202 (716) 846–4301

180 State St., Room 412, Elmira, NY 14904 (607) 733–4686

99 Washington Ave., Twin Towers Bldg., Room 922, Albany, NY 12210 (518) 472–6300

Region 3

109 North 3d St., Rm. 301, Lowndes Bldg., Clarksburg, WV 26301 (304) 623–5361

Federal Bldg., 1000 Liberty Ave., Rm. 1401, Pittsburgh, PA 15222 (412) 644–2780

Federal Bldg., 400 North 8th St., Rm. 3015, Richmond, VA 23240 (703) 782–2618

1030 15th St., N.W., 2nd Fl., Washington, DC 20417 (202) 655–4000

100 Chestnut Street, Harrisburg, PA 17101 (717) 782–3840

20 N. Pennsylvania Ave., Wilkes-Barre, PA 18702 (717) 826–6497

844 King St., Federal Bldg., Rm. 5207, Wilmington, Del. 19801 (302) 573–6294

8600 LaSalle Rd., Towson, Md. 21204 (301) 962–4392

Region 4

908 South 20th St., Rm. 202, Birmingham, AL 35205 (205) 254–1344

230 S. Tryon St., Addison Bldg., Charlotte, NC 29202 (704) 372–0711

1801 Assembly St., Rm. 117, Columbia, SC 29201 (803) 765–5376

Petroleum Bldg., Suite 690, 200 Pascagoula St., Jackson, MS 39201 (601) 969–4371

Federal Bldg., 400 West Bay St., Rm. 261, Jacksonville, FL 32202 (904) 791–3782

2222 Ponce de Leon Blvd., 5th Floor, Miami, FL 33184 (305) 350–5521

404 James Robertson Pkwy., Nashville, TN 37219 (615) 251–5881

502 South Gay St., Rm. 307, Fidelity Bankers Bldg., Knoxville, TN 37902 (615) 637–9300

215 South Evans St., Greenville, NC 27834 (919) 752–3798

111 Fred Haise Blvd., Gulf Nat. Life Ins. Bldg., 2nd Fl., Biloxi, MS (601) 435–3676

700 Twiggs St., Suite 607, Tampa, FL 33602 (813) 228–2594

Federal Bldg., 167 North Main St., Rm. 211, Memphis, TN 38103 (901) 521–3588

Region 5

One North Old State Capital Plaza, Springfield, IL 62701 (217) 525–4416

1240 East 9th St., Rm. 317, Cleveland, OH 44199 (216) 522–4180

85 Marconi Blvd., Columbus, OH 43215 (614) 469–6860

Federal Bldg., 550 Main St., Cincinnati, OH 45202 (513) 684–2814

477 Michigan Ave., McNamara Bldg., Detroit, MI 48226 (313) 226–6075

575 N. Pennsylvania Ave., Century Bldg., Indianapolis, IN 46204 (317) 269–7272

212 East Washington Ave., Rm. 552, Madison, WI 53703 (608) 252–5261

12 South 6th St., Plymouth Bldg., Minneapolis, MN 55402 (612) 625–2362

540 W. Kaye Ave., Marquette, MI 49855 (906) 225–1108

Federal Bldg., 517 East Wisconsin Ave., Room 246, Milwaukee, WI 53202 (414) 291–3941

500 South Barstow St., Rm. 16, Fed. Off. Bldg, & U.S. Courthouse, Eau Claire, WI 54701 (715) 834–9012

Region 6

5000 Marble Ave., N.E., Patio Plaza Bldg., Albuquerque, NM 87110 (505) 766–3430

One Allen Ctr., 500 Dallas, Houston, TX 77002 (713) 226–4341

611 Gaines St., Suite 900, Little Rock, AR 72201 (501) 378–5871

1205 Texas Ave., Lubbock, TX 79408 (806) 762–7011

222 East Van Buren St., Harlingen, TX 78550 (Lower Rio Grande Valley) (512) 423–8934

1000 South Washington St., Marshall, TX 75670 (214) 935–5257

Plaza Tower, 17th Floor, 1011 Howard Ave., New Orleans, LA 70113 (504) 589–2611

200 N.W. 5th St., Suite 670, Oklahoma City, OK 73102 (405) 231–4301

727 E. Durango, Rm. A-513, San Antonio, TX 78206 (512) 229–6250

1100 Commerce St., Rm. 300, Dallas, TX 75202 (214) 749–3961

4100 Rio Bravo, Suite 300, El Paso, TX 79902 (915) 543–7200

3105 Leopard St., Corpus Christi, TX 78408 (512) 888–3011

Region 7

New Federal Bldg., 210 Walnut St., Rm. 749, Des Moines, IA 50309 (515) 284–4422

19th and Farnam Sts., Empire State Bldg., Omaha, NE 68102 (402) 221–4691

Suite 2500 Mercantile Tower, St. Louis, MO 63101 (314) 425–4191

110 East Waterman, Wichita, KA 67202 (316) 267–6311

Region 8

Rm. 4001, Federal Bldg., 100 East B St., Casper, WY 82601 (307) 265–5550

301 S. Park, Rm. 528, Helena, MT 59601 (406) 449–5381

Federal Bldg., 657 2d Ave., North, Rm. 218, Fargo, ND 58102 (701) 237–5771

Federal Bldg., 125 South State St., Rm. 2237, Salt Lake City, UT 84111 (801) 524–5800

National Bank Bldg., 8th and Maine Ave., Rm. 402, Sioux Falls, SD 57102 (605) 336–2980

515 9th St., Federal Bldg., Rapid City, SD 57701 (605) 343–5074

Region 9

300 Ala Moana, Honolulu, HI (808) 546–8950

350 S. Figueroa St., Los Angeles, CA 90071 (213) 688–2956

3030 North Central Ave., Phoenix, AZ 85012 (602) 261–3611

880 Front St., Rm. 4-5-33, San Diego, CA 92101 (714) 293–5440

301 E. Stewart, Las Vegas, NV 89121 (702) 385–6011

1229 N St., Fresno, CA 93721 (209) 487–5000

Region 10

1016 West 6th Ave., Suite 200, Anchorage Legal Center, Anchorage, AK 99501 (907) 272–5561

101 12th Ave., Fairbanks, AK 99701 (907) 452–1951

1005 Main St., Boise, ID 83701 (208) 384–1096.

1220 S.W. Third Ave., Portland, OR 97205 (503) 221–2682

Court House Bldg., Rm. 651, Spokane, WA 99210 (509) 452–2100

Franchising Organizations

Two franchising organizations can also provide you with further information. One is the International Franchise Association, founded in 1960. This organization, which stands for ethical franchise operations, publishes a guide to franchising. Its members must follow a strict code of behavior (listed in Chapter 5). You have a better chance of dealing with a franchise that's on the level if it's a member of this organization. For more information write:

International Franchise Association
1025 Connecticut Avenue, NW
Suite 1005
Washington, DC 20036

Another franchising organization is the National Franchise Coalition, founded by a group of franchisees in 1975. It is dedicated to providing support for franchisees. It has done a great deal of research on franchising and has a knowledgeable legal committee. You may want to join or ask advice. Write to:

National Franchise Coalition
P.O. Box 366
Fox Lake, Illinois 60020

Chapter 7

Money and the Franchise

*Financial Facts / Purchasing the Franchise /
Finding the Money*

THIS CHAPTER deals with several of the problems encountered in financing a franchise. First, it shows you how you can judge your potential sales and costs, another safety check of the franchise you plan to buy. Second, it describes how to buy a franchise. And third, it shows you where and how you can get the money.

Financial Facts

Your franchisor will provide you with financial statements and estimate your costs and potential profits. It's up to you to verify these facts.

First, as mentioned before, you can't take for granted the start-up costs the franchisor claims. You must carefully log what your money needs will be. Include the cost of the franchise, your operating expenses for the first year, and the money you'll need personally for an additional year. It's far better to overestimate than underestimate. In an age when 80 percent of small businesses fail in the first 3 years, you can be sure many of those failures were due to underestimating costs while overestimating sales. Franchises usually do far better than independent small businesses. However, it still takes over a year and even up to 2 years before you are likely to show any real profits.

How do you go about finding out how much money you need? The franchisor supplies the information about the franchise fee and royalties. The SBA can be questioned about a particular business's sales information. You can also check with the local chamber of commerce. And don't forget your fellow franchisees. They should provide you with a wealth of information about costs. Question them closely about the relationship of the franchisor's estimates to the real costs.

The following are some of the specific areas that will cost you money:

- *The franchise fee.* What you pay for the right to use the franchise name and conduct the business under that name. Some franchises refund this if the franchise meets or exceeds its quota.
- *Additional franchise charges.* Inventories; construction materials.
- *Services.* Expert instruction and initial help; accounting services.
- *Equipment and fixtures.* From furniture to grills and refrigerators.
- *Labor.* Employee salaries.
- *Franchise royalties.* Monthly payments of between 5 and 10 percent of your gross.
- *Other.* Benefits, insurance, taxes, and so on.

You should have your accountant take a look at the figures for the franchise's projected income and expenses. If it all adds up, fine. If not, ask the franchisor why not. In all probability, there are regional variations in both income and costs, and what you are looking at is an average.

Probably the most difficult area to estimate is what your own personal costs will be. You have to take the time to do this carefully and honestly. Don't keep cutting here and there until your budget barely allows you to starve.

Study your family expenses. Break down medical, clothing, food, entertainment, and other costs into monthly listings. This tells you how much you need to have available to pay your current bills and keep your head above water.

Now that you know how much you need to spend, try to determine how much you'll be able to make. This isn't really a separate step, but part of the process of determining costs. Again your primary sources will be the SBA, chamber of commerce, and fellow franchisees. Is your return enough? After you take out your salary, will you have any profit? Will your business be able to grow? If the answer is no, you're looking at the wrong business.

Purchasing the Franchise

How do you buy into a franchise? It may appear simple at first, but there are a few stumbling blocks—unless you have all the capital you need.

You may be under the impression that it isn't as hard to get money for franchising as for a private business. In many cases, this is quite true. With established franchises, you have an entity that can be studied, checked, and double-checked by loan officers. The established franchise can open many doors for you that would undoubtedly have been closed if you had not had the franchise organization behind you.

Also, some franchises still do offer to finance a part of your package. Some franchises in these days of tight money are also helping to put together very creative financing packages. However, in most instances, the franchisor will leave some of the dirty work up to you. And in many cases, the franchisor will also demand a hefty amount of the initial start-up cost in cash.

The first step is to see what the prospective franchise

charges. You'll note in the examples at the end of the book what is referred to as equity capital. This doesn't represent the total investment, but what the company estimates is the minimal amount of money you'll need to start the business.

Franchise costs vary tremendously. Some require equity capital of half a million dollars and more; others, just a couple thousand of dollars. What is included in this cost? First, the franchise fee. Second, the various charges associated with building the business. Third, miscellaneous expenses, which vary depending upon the type of business.

Finding the Money

So how do you get the money? First, you'll have to have a certain amount of cash up front. This varies, depending upon the type of business. Most franchisors like their franchisees to invest a good chunk of their own money in the venture. They also approve of borrowing money from relatives—a major source of capital in many businesses.

Of course, relatives must be treated scrupulously just like anyone else. Make sure they don't attach strings to any loans and won't try to capriciously ask you to pay them back.

Your franchisor also may help you out in financing your business. Some provide low-interest loans as long as you have invested a good chunk of your own money. In most cases, however, you probably won't be able to get a direct loan from the franchise organization. But the franchise organization is good for more than giving out a loan, it's also an extremely good reference for obtaining a loan from a bank or other source.

The franchisor will arm you with some very impressive records when you go to see your banker. It isn't just you who is being examined, but the whole franchise organization. If your franchise has a good reputation, the bank officer will certainly consider you sooner than if you had come in on your own.

The Small Business Administration may also be a viable source of money. It's generally a last resort situation that drives a businessman to the SBA, but this organization has made thousands of business loans. Loan processing is drawn out, but it certainly is worth it. Contact your local office for more information. (See the list of SBA offices in Chapter 6.)

Another funding option for prospective franchisees is to form a partnership. Finding another person to shoulder some of the expenses and liabilities can be very attractive. Some franchise organizations even encourage partnerships.

However, the drawbacks to a partnership are obvious. You are wedded to another individual in a business venture. If one wants out, what then? If you can't buy your partner out, you're forced to sell the business, perhaps before you want to. There are also the human factors to consider. Will you be able to get along with this person day in day out? If you're not compatible to start with, you had better try another tactic; this one just isn't going to work out.

Financing your franchise is part of the equation you've been working on since you first decided to buy a small business. By this stage, you've determined how much you need, how much you can afford, and where to get the money. If they all match up and the franchisor accepts you as one of the family, you're in luck. If not, lower your sights and aim for something more realistic. Just because you weren't able to buy into a McDonald's or a Holiday Inn, doesn't mean that you can't afford something smaller.

Chapter 8

Checklist and Worksheet

PART I ENDS with a checklist and worksheet developed by the SBA. These are excellent guides for you to follow. If you can't answer yes to any of the questions on the checklist that directly pertain to your franchise, you had better try to remedy that situation. The worksheet is there for you to expand upon the checklist. Put down the specifics on the worksheet. Since you'll certainly want to check out more than one franchise, you can duplicate this worksheet and use one copy for each franchise you investigate.

Questions To Answer Affirmatively Before Going into Franchising

*Check if
answer
is "yes"*

The Franchisor

1. Has the franchisor been in business long enough (5 years or more) to have established a good reputation? _____

2. Have you checked Better Business Bureaus, chambers of commerce, Dun and Bradstreet, or bankers to find out about the franchisor's business reputation and credit rating? _____

3. Did the above investigations reveal that the franchisor has a good reputation and credit rating? _____

4. Does the franchising firm appear to be financed adequately so that it can carry out its stated plan of financial assistance and expansion? _____

5. Have you found out how many franchisees are now operating? _____

6. Have you found out the "mortality" or failure rate among franchisees? _____

7. Is the failure rate small?

8. Have you checked with some franchisees and found that the franchisor has a reputation for honesty and fair dealing among those who currently hold franchises? _____

9. Has the franchisor shown you certified figures indicating exact net profits of one or more going operations which you have personally checked yourself? _____

10. Has the franchisor given you a specimen contract to study with the advice of your legal counsel? _____

11. Will the franchisor assist you with:
    a. A management training program? _____
    b. An employee training program? _____
    c. A public relations program? _____
    d. Obtaining capital? _____
    e. Good credit terms? _____
    f. Merchandising ideas? _____
    g. Designing store layout and displays? _____
    h. Inventory control methods? _____
    i. Analyzing financial statements? _____

12. Does the franchisor provide continuing assistance for franchisees through supervisors who visit regularly? _____

13. Does the franchising firm have an experienced management trained in depth? _____

14. Will the franchisor assist you in finding a good location for your business? _____

15. Has the franchising company investigated *you* carefully enough to assure itself that you can successfully operate one of its franchises at a profit both to it and to you? _____

16. Have you determined exactly what the franchisor can do for you that you cannot do for yourself? _____

The Product or Service

17. Has the product or service been on the market long enough to gain good consumer acceptance? _____

18. Is it priced competitively? _____

19. Is it the type of item or service that the same consumer customarily buys more than once? _____
20. Is it an all-year seller in contrast to a seasonal one? _____
21. Is it a staple item in contrast to a fad? _____
22. Does it sell well elsewhere? _____
23. Would you buy it on its merits? _____
24. Will it be in greater demand 5 years from now? _____
25. If it is a product rather than a service:
    a. Is it packaged attractively? _____
    b. Does it stand up well in use? _____
    c. Is it easy and safe to use? _____
    d. Is it patented? _____
    e. Does it comply with all applicable laws? _____
    f. Is it manufactured under certain quality standards? _____
    g. Do these standards compare favorably with similar products on the market? _____
    h. If the product must be purchased exclusively from the franchisor or a designated supplier, are the prices to you, as the franchisee, competitive? _____

The Franchise Contract

26. Does the franchise fee seem reasonable? _____
27. Do continuing royalties or percent of gross sales payment appear reasonable? _____
28. Is the total cash investment required and the terms for financing the balance satisfactory? _____
29. Does the cash investment include payment for fixtures and equipment? _____
30. If you will be required to participate in company sponsored promotion and publicity by contributing to an "advertising fund," will you have the right to veto any increase in contributions to the "fund?" _____
31. If the parent company's product or service is protected by patent or liability insurance, is the same protection extended to you? _____
32. Are you free to buy the amount of merchandise you believe you need rather than being required to purchase a certain amount? _____
33. Can you, as the franchisee, return merchandise for credit? _____
34. Can you engage in other business activities? _____

35. If there is an annual sales quota, can you retain your franchise if it is not met? _____

36. Does the contract give you an exclusive territory for the length of the franchise? _____

37. Is your territory protected? _____

38. Is the franchise agreement renewable? _____

39. Can you terminate your agreement if you are not happy for some reason? _____

40. Is the franchisor prohibited from selling the franchise out from under you? _____

41. May you sell the business to whomever you please? _____

42. If you sell your franchise, will you be compensated for the goodwill you have built into the business? _____

43. Does the contract obligate the franchisor to give you continuing assistance after you are operating the business? _____

44. Are you permitted a choice in determining whether you will sell any new product or service introduced by the franchisor after you have opened your business? _____

45. Is there anything with respect to the franchise or its operation that would make you ineligible for special financial assistance or other benefits accorded to small business concerns by federal, state, or local governments? _____

46. Did your lawyer approve the franchise contract after he studied it paragraph by paragraph? _____

47. Is the contract free and clear of requirements that would call upon you to take any steps that are, according to your lawyer, unwise or illegal in your state, county, or city? _____

48. Does the contract cover all aspects of your agreement with the franchisor? _____

49. Does it really benefit both you and the franchisor? _____

Your Market

50. Are the territorial boundaries of your market completely, accurately, and understandably defined? _____

51. Have you made any study to determine whether the product or service you propose to sell has a market in your territory at the prices you will have to charge? _____

52. Does the territory provide an adequate sales potential? _____

53. Will the population in the territory given you increase over the next 5 years? _____

54. Will the average per capita income in the territory remain the same or increase over the next 5 years? _____

55. Is existing competition in your territory for the product or service not too well entrenched? _____

YOU—The Franchisee

56. Do you know where you are going to get the equity capital you will need? _____

57. Have you compared what it would take to start your own similar business with the price you must pay for the franchise? _____

58. Have you made a business plan—for example:
    a. Have you worked out what income from sales or services you can reasonably expect in the first 6 months? The first year? The second year? _____
    b. Have you made a forecast of expenses including a regular salary for yourself? _____

59. Are you prepared to give up some independence of action to secure the advantages offered by the franchise? _____

60. Are you capable of accepting supervision, even though you will presumably be your own boss? _____

61. Are you prepared to accept rules and regulations with which you may not agree? _____

62. Can you afford the period of training involved? _____

63. Are you ready to spend much or all of the remainder of your business life with this franchisor, offering his product or service to the public? _____

Franchise Index/Profile

A. Franchise—General

1. Is the product or service:

	yes	no
a. Considered reputable		
b. Part of a growing market		
c. Needed in your area		
d. Of interest to you		
e. Safe		
Protected		
Covered by guarantee		
f. Carry the name of a well known personality		
Sound franchise without well known personality		

2. Is the franchise: *yes no*
   a. Local   ___ ___
      Regional   ___ ___
      National   ___ ___
      International   ___ ___
   b. Full time   ___ ___
      Part time   ___ ___
      Full time possible in future   ___ ___

3. Existing franchises
   a. How long was the company in business before the first franchise was awarded? ___ years.
   b. What date was the company founded and what date was the first franchise awarded? Company founded ___. First franchise awarded ___.
   c. Number currently in operation or under construction? ___. Information on those to contact:

   Franchise 1: Owner_____

                  Address_____

                  _____

                  Telephone_____

                  Date Started_____

   Franchise 2: Owner_____

                  Address_____

                  _____

                  Telephone_____

                  Date started_____

   Franchise 3: Owner_____

                  Address_____

                  _____

                  Telephone_____

Date Started_____

Franchise 4: Owner_____

Address_____

_____

Telephone_____

Date Started_____

    d. How many franchises are planned for the next 12 months (not including those awarded and not yet in operation)? ____.

4. Why have franchises failed?
    a. How many franchises have failed?____How many of these have been in the last 2 years?
    b. Why have franchises failed?

Franchisor Reasons:_____

_____

_____

Better Business Bureau Reasons:_____

_____

_____

Franchisee:_____

_____

_____

5. Franchise in local market area
    Has a franchise ever been awarded in this area?_____
    If so and if it is still in operation:

Owner_____

Address_____

Telephone_____ Date started _____

If so and if it is no longer in operation:

Person involved_____

Address_____

Date Started_____ Date ended_____

Reasons for failure_____

_____

How many inquiries have you had for your franchise from my area in the past 6 months?____.

6. What product or service will be added to the franchise package?

    a. Within 12 months?_____

    _____

    b. Within 2 years?_____

    _____

    c. Within 2 to 5 years?_____

    _____

7. Competition

    What is my competition?_____

_____

_____

8. Are all franchises independently owned?
   a. Of the total outlets, _____ are franchised, and _____ are company owned.
   b. If some outlets are company owned did they start out this way _____ or were they repurchased from a franchisee _____. Date of most recent company acquisition _____.

9. Franchise distribution pattern
   a. Is the franchise exclusive _____ or nonexclusive _____.
   b. Is the franchise a distributorship _____ or a dealership _____. If it is a dealership who is the distributor in my area:

   Name_____

   Address_____

   How long has he been a distributor?_____

10. Franchise operations
    a. and b. What facilities are required and do I lease or build. Operated out of home _____

	Build	*Lease*
Office		
Building		
Manufacturing facility		
Warehouse		

    c. and d. Getting started . . . who is responsible for what?

	Franchisor	*Franchisee*
Feasibility Study		
Design		
Construction		
Furnishing		
Financing		

B. Franchise Company

1. What is the name and address of the parent company if different from the franchise company:

    Name_____

    Address_____

2. Is the parent company public ____ or private ____

3. If the company is public where is the stock traded:

    New York Stock Exchange

    American Stock Exchange   _____

    Over the Counter   _____

    _____   _____

4. If the company is private the president is _____. The following bank can be used as a reference:

    Name_____

    Address_____

    Person to contact_____

C. Financial And Legal Advice

1. Where to get advice:
    a. Lawyer

        Name_____

        Address_____

        Telephone_____

    b. Financial

        Name_____

        Address_____

        Telephone_____

c. Management

Name_____

Address_____

Telephone_____

2. Total franchise cost
   a. How much money do I have to have to get started?

Item	Amount
Franchise start up	$_____
First year operating	$_____
First year personal	$_____
TOTAL	$_____

   b. What do I have to pay the franchisor to get started? $_____
      Basis of cost:

Item	Amount
Franchise fee	$_____
Services	$_____
Product	$_____
Real estate	$_____
Equipment	$_____
_____	$_____

   c. Is any of the initial franchise cost refundable?_____.

   If so, on what basis?_____

   _____

3. Financing
    a. Is part of the initial cost to the franchisee financed? ____. If so, how much? $ ____. This represents ____% of the total initial cost.
    b. What is the interest rate? ____ %. When does financing have to be paid back? ____

4. Forecast of income and expenses
    a. Is a forecast of income and expenses provided? ____.
       Is it:
       based on actual franchisee operations? ____
       based on a franchisor outlet? ____
       purely estimated? ____
       If a forecast is provided does it:

	yes	no
b. Relate to your market area		
c. Meet your personal goals		
d. Provide adequate return on investment		
e. Provide for adequate promotion and personnel		

5. What is the best legal structure for my company?
    a. Proprietorship _____
    b. Partnership _____
    c. Corporation _____

6. Are all details covered in a written franchise contract?
    Yes ____ No ____ (get copy for lawyer and accountant review)
    a. What to look for—are these included:

	yes	no
Franchise fee		
Termination		
Selling and renewal		
Advertising and promotion		
Patent and liability protection		
Home office services		
Commissions and royalties		
Training		
Financing		
Territory		
Exclusive vs. nonexclusive		

D. *Training*

1. Initial training
   a. Does franchisor provide formal initial training? _____.
      If so how long does it last? _____.

   b. Cost

	yes	no
Included in franchise cost		
Includes all materials		
Includes transportation		
Includes room and board		

   If not included in franchise cost what is total cost including all outlined above? $_____.

   c. What does the training course include?

	yes	no
Franchise operations		
Sales		
Finance		
Promotion		
Personnel		
Management		
Manufacturing and maintenance		
Training		

   d. How do you train your initial staff? Is a training program provided? _____. Does the franchisor make available a staff member from the home office to assist? _____. What materials are included in the staff training program?_____

   _____

   _____

2. Continuing training
   What is the continuing program? Is there any cost? _____. If so, how much? $ _____. Are there any special materials or equipment required? _____. If so what? _____. What is the cost to the franchisee? $ _____.

E. Marketing

1. How is the product or service sold?

	yes	no
In home—appointment		
In home—cold		
Telephone		
In store or place of business		
At business—appointment		
At business—cold		
Mail		

2. How do you get the sales leads?

	yes	no
Franchisor		
Franchisee		
Both		
Advertising		
Direct mail		
Telephone		
Trade shows		

3. Who are the prospects for the products or services? Outline a brief

   profile:_____

   _____

4. What is the national advertising program of the franchisor?
   a. What is the national advertising budget?
      $____.
   b. What are the primary advertising media?
      Television ____
      Radio ____
      Outdoor ____
      Newspaper ____
      Magazine ____
      Direct mail ____

5. What kind of advertising and promotion support is available for the
   local franchisee?

	yes	no
Is a packaged advertising program available?	————	————
Is there a co-op advertising program?	————	————
Is there a grand opening package?	————	————

6. Should you have an advertising agency?————.

F. Home Office Support

1. Principals and directors
   a. Who are the key persons in the day to day operation of the business?

name	title	background
————	————	————
————	————	————
————	————	————
————	————	————
————	————	————

   b. Who are the directors (do not include those from a. above)?

name	business association
————	————
————	————
————	————

2. Consultants
   a. Who are the consultants to the company?

name   *business specialty*

_____   _____

_____   _____

_____   _____

3. Service departments

	yes	no
What service departments do you have?		
Finance and accounting		
Advertising and promotion		
Sales and marketing		
Research and development		
Real estate		
Construction		
Personnel and training		
Manufacturing and operations		
Purchasing		
_____		
_____		

4. Field support
Do you have a field man assigned to working with a set number of franchises? ____
Who would be assigned to my franchise? ____
How many other franchises is he assigned to? ____
May I contact him? ____

Part II

Running Your Franchise

FRANCHISORS DIFFER GREATLY in the amount of aid they give to their franchisees. Some franchisors retain a great deal more control over their franchisees than others. All some do is to sell a trademark, hand over a manual, and tell you you're on your own. Others provide cradle-to-grave advice and help.

This section serves as a reference to those franchisors that offer substantial help to the franchisee and as an important aid to those who find that you must rely more upon yourself. The subjects covered here include:

- Choosing a location for your business
- Selecting employees
- Management techniques
- Promotion and advertising
- Bookkeeping procedures

Chapter 9

Choosing the Right Location

THE LOCATION of your franchise is often left up to you. Many franchises will counsel you in choosing the proper site for your business and will reject your selection if it is obviously unsuitable. However, you should be aware yourself of what makes a good business location.

It isn't always immediately apparent why one site does well and another site does poorly. There are many considerations.

Deceived by Appearances

Harry wanted to start a fried chicken franchise on a busy stretch of highway in his hometown. There already were several fast-food restaurants along that stretch, and they appeared to being doing well. Harry thought another restaurant along that stretch would be a sure thing. So Harry convinced the franchisor, built his restaurant, and settled down to business. Unfortunately, he soon discovered that he didn't have a sure thing. He only barely eked out a living for a couple of years and then had to close his doors.

The problem was that the area Harry selected had reached the saturation point for fast-food businesses. The competition was too intense, and there just wasn't enough traffic to support everyone. Harry made the mistake of poor-

ly estimating what his business would be. He didn't solidly
research the site. Especially, he didn't talk with the owners
or managers of the other restaurants to see how they were
actually doing—not how they appeared to be doing.

Competition is one thing to worry about; the taste of the
community is another. It helps to do a little demographic
study of the area where you want to set up a business, so go
beyond what the franchisor will do for you. Ask yourself
what kind of customers you are attempting to sell to. If your
service or product is aimed chiefly at the relatively young
and affluent, forget about opening your franchise in a retirement area.

Of course all franchises should be located in sections of the
country that can afford them, but certain communities are
more receptive to specific franchises than others. For example, a well-to-do suburban location would better support a
lawn care operation than an urban or even a rural area. On
the other hand, a recreation vehicle franchise may do quite
well in a more rural area.

In most cases, your franchisor will offer some guidance on
these considerations, but you need to understand the basics
of your business yourself to get that extra edge. You want to
be in charge of a business that does superbly instead of
managing one that just squeaks by.

Here are several other items to investigate when looking
for the ideal location:

- *What kind of neighborhood surrounds the site?* It
  makes eminent sense in this day and age to consider and
  reconsider locating your business in any high crime
  area. It's certainly possible to make a great deal of
  money in certain trouble spots—convenience stores
  often do fair business in poor areas—but you may not
  care to be robbed every week.
- *Do you like the location?* Your franchise is your business, your home away from home. You'll often put 60

hours and more each week at your business. If you don't like the area or the people, you've got a problem, one that may translate into the loss of business because of a bad attitude and lack of rapport with customers. Even if you made a good living, would you want to stay in a place that you dislike?

- *What about the future of the location?* It may look good now, but what will it be like in 5 or 10 years? This is difficult, but try to project what the surrounding community will be like in the years to come. Is the neighborhood growing or declining? Is unemployment rising or falling? It doesn't make much sense to open a business in an area that might get progressively poorer. In some cases that is unavoidable. Franchisees who have set up operations in towns that rely upon the auto industry have often taken a beating along with the rest of the local businesses.

- *Can you get adequate help?* If you need skilled workers, you have to consider where they're going to come from. There has to be a local labor pool that you can tap.

- *Can your customers find you easily?* You should be located on the pulse of the community, not off in the backwoods somewhere.

- *How does the location compare to others in your immediate area?* This is a catch-all. For example, what is the price of land or the rental in one town as compared to another? What about the zoning laws? How's the garbage pick-up (an important consideration for a fast-food restaurant)?

In short, when you add up all the pluses and minuses, does the location you've selected still make sense? If it does, congratulations. If not, you've saved yourself a good deal of grief by knowing where you shouldn't put your business.

Again, it's a matter of applying yourself and doing some legwork. If your franchisor's headquarters are in Miami, and you want to open a franchise in New Haven, do yourself a favor and go beyond company recommendations. Chances are, you'll be able to get a better feel for where you want to locate than the franchisor could.

The franchisor's representatives will be on the lookout for any gross mistakes, but you should be aware of the subtle ebbs and flows of the community. It takes work, but the better prepared you are, the fewer mistakes you'll make—and the more solid your franchise will be.

Some specific steps you can take include looking over the competition and contacting other franchisees. In the course of your talking with other franchisees, try to learn what makes one tremendously successful and another less so. Be on the lookout for ideas you too can use. Ask about the franchisee's selection of the site. How did he or she make the decision? What were some of the key factors that led them to their location?

After you've checked with the franchisees, study the competition and other businesses in the vicinity of your possible site. Some of the owners will talk to you, some won't. But the consensus should give you a rough idea of the business volume.

Another way to check business volume is to hang around and watch it. Estimate the number of customers that competitors have at peak time. Spend a few hours at various times of the day studying the traffic flow around the stores to see what you can expect. Take into account the day of the week and the time of the year. You should be able to project what the volume will be like and whether the busy times and quiet times indicate a poor, fair, or prime location.

Chapter 10

Hiring Employees

The Job Description / How to Find Applicants /
Making the Selection

MANY FRANCHISES offer guidance in this area, but the more you yourself understand about the process, the better off you'll be in the end.

Hiring employees can be complicated—as is anything that involves dealing with people. But basically you have a simple goal—to hire the best person for the job.

There are a few pitfalls to avoid in your quest for the perfect employee—an employee who works well, who won't steal you blind, someone you can trust. Too many employers, to their immense regret, paid too little attention to proper hiring methods.

"We only need a high school girl to operate the cash register. We'll just put a sign in the window." If you aren't careful, the sweet little girl who walked in off the street can drain a substantial amount of money from your operation. Many businesses have failed because of the flagrant dishonesty of their employees. Many more have failed because their employees were always late, were generally careless, and made a bad impression on the customers.

There's a wrong way and a right way to look for people. The wrong way is to put a sign in the window and accept the first person who seems qualified. It is also wrong to hire on hunches or first impressions. And it is very wrong to treat the hiring process as if it were of little importance in the scheme of your business—because it isn't.

Your employees are as much a part of your franchise as you are. They have a stake in the franchise's operations, just as you do. Like you, they often represent your business to customers. Their attitudes and approach to work are extremely important.

The Job Description

To find the right employee, you have to know all about the position to be filled. Often, the franchisor provides a job description that helps you match the employee to the job. If not, make up your own job description. This is an important step. First of all, you must understand the job to be performed so you can manage it well. Second, the job description provides a written profile for the employee to follow. With a good job description, he or she has an initial jump on the job. If it's all written down, it's much easier to comprehend.

A job description has two parts: first, logically enough, a description of the actual job and what it entails; and second, the job specification. This provides you with a list of the qualifications your employee should have.

A sample job description for a short-order cook might look like this:

Position: Short-order cook
Supervisor: Restaurant manager
Duties:

- Operates grill
- Operates french fryer
- Prepares sandwiches
- Cleans area
- Maintains high level of sanitation

- Helps with other duties—maintains cold room, takes orders, serves customers
- Works on other tasks assigned by manager

Job specifications:

- *Education:* High school graduate preferred.
- *Experience:* One year preferred; will consider a trainee.
- *Skills:* Must be able to operate a grill; work well under rush hour pressure; have good, basic mathematical comprehension for both cash register and portion control.
- *Other:* Vital that he or she is neat and clean and knows about sanitation.

This is just a simple blueprint. You would want to add substantially more to this job description since you know the specific duties.

If you need more help, the government publishes a useful source called the *Dictionary of Occupational Titles*, which is almost certainly in your local library's reference section. This work has two volumes. The first volume lists the actual definitions of various worker's duties and provides a good overview of occupations. Volume Two goes into more detail; it groups related jobs and classifies the abilities, vocational experience, and potential of workers. It also includes a qualifications profile that may be useful when you write up job specifications.

How to Find Applicants

Once you've developed the job description, you'll be able to start looking for people who fit the bill. The big question is how to find them? There are several ways to go about this. Here are a few:

Employment Agencies.   Among private agencies, there are good ones and bad ones. Ask around. Try to get a feel for the people you'll be doing business with. Make a few phone calls to other local businesses and see if they recommend any particular agency.

There are also government-run agencies. These agencies used to have a bad reputation, since some of their clients seemed more interested in staying on the public dole than in obtaining work. However, many state agencies have extremely good records in placing excellent people—especially in the lower level and blue collar jobs. Another plus is that these agencies are free, whereas either you or your employee would have to pay for the private agency.

When using an employment agency, you must remain part of the hiring process. Don't accept the first candidate. Try to get several applicants so you can compare them. It may be that the agency was totally right in its first selection, but maybe it wasn't.

You might be interested to know that a substantial number of private employment agencies are themselves franchises. See Part III.

Advertising. Your franchisor may help you out here. If not, there are a few tricks to remember. First, you have to write the ad. This isn't as simple as it sounds. If the ad isn't clear, you may get responses from hundreds of people who aren't at all qualified.

A help wanted ad that merely states the following may not be very helpful:

Wanted: Short-order cook. Contact Mr. Henderson

It isn't specific enough. The following would work better:

Wanted: Short-order cook with min. 2 years experience. Evenings, 4 days a week. Contact Mr. Henderson.

This ad provides more specific information and also informs prospective applicants that the hours are irregular and that they must have experience.

Depending on how much you want to spend, you can

order a large ad that leaps off the page or a small two- or three-line ad. It's up to you. In a tight job market, like the one we're in right now, job hunters pay attention to all ads, not just the jazzed-up ones.

The next step is placing your ad. You may just want to put it in your local paper, but if it's for an important position, you may even want to advertise outside of your area. Some advertisers wait for a Sunday edition, which generally contains a larger help wanted section.

You also don't have to stop at newspapers. Journals and trade publications are useful hunting grounds. The only problem with some of these publications is that most are monthly, so you would have to wait for a while before you obtained any responses.

Schools. This includes high schools, colleges, trade schools, and vocational schools. Unless you hire someone from a work-study program, you'll be dealing with novices, so you should realize that these people have to be handled differently from experienced employees. They generally have to be guided a bit more.

If you're interested, contact an institution's guidance counselor or career development department for further information.

Employee Referrals. A valued employee may have a good idea where to find someone. But this presents a problem in itself. If the referral doesn't work out, your present employee may feel slighted.

Walk-ins. You can't depend on walk-ins, but you shouldn't disregard them either. In all probability you won't have a position available right then, but take a few minutes to talk to them anyway. If they seem good, you may want to take their names and credentials and call them when you do have an opening.

Organizations for the Handicapped and Disabled. You may want to check with any local organizations. They often can provide excellent people for jobs. You may be surprised at the level of skill and dedication many of these people can bring with them to the job.

Situation-Wanted Ads. All you have to do is glance through a newspaper or trade journal, and you're bound to find several of these ads. They cost you no money, obviously, so if you read about someone with the background you want, call him or her—it may work out.

Temporary help. Agencies that specialize in temporary jobs are used by thousands of businesses across the country. You may not need a full-time employee, or you may need a full-time employee for only a few weeks or months. That is when the temporary agencies can serve you well.

As you did with the other personnel agencies, take some time to find the best one. In fact, they may be one and the same, for many employment agencies offer both full-time and temporary help.

Retirees. Retired people can be a fine source of labor. They often have a great deal of experience and can offer excellent advice in day-to-day operations.

Family and Relatives. A large proportion of small franchise owners wouldn't be in business if it weren't for their families. With relatives, you at least know where you stand—at least most of the time. You usually don't have to worry about whether or not your niece is telling you the truth about her background. Working with your relatives is a subject in itself, and it is covered at the end of Chapter 11.

Making the Selection

You now have to plunge ahead and hire someone. By this time, and through whatever sources, you should have at least a handful of people to consider. They will have filled out an *application form*—an important step, since it provides you with the basic information about the applicant. Your franchise probably has a standard application form. If not, see the sample application form on page 88.

The completed application form tells you some things about the person who filled it out. First, it tells you whether he or she can follow instructions, can read and write and comprehend—not a small point these days. Second, it indicates which applicants are *not* suitable. If they don't meet your qualifications as outlined on the application, they can be eliminated. Since you can't take anything for granted, an applicant who does appear qualified has passed only the first step. Everything has to be carefully checked.

The amount of time you spend looking for an employee depends to a large degree on the skill level you need. An assistant manager takes more time to find than a busboy. But, the busboy should be checked out just as well.

At this point, applicants are only pieces of paper or recommendations—not people you have met face to face. So it is time to meet with the applicants.

This is the *interview process.* And this is where you get an initial understanding of the person or persons who might eventually work for you. The interview should be well thought out in advance. You should have a list of specific questions to ask, a body of facts to gather. Take notes during the interview, perhaps have a checklist to help you distinguish this applicant from all the rest.

It isn't easy. You're attempting to discover several things about this stranger that can help you to decide whether you want to offer this particular applicant a job. Remember, this person may become extremely important to you. You'll probably be working closely with him or her, and at times may even be trusting the business to his or her expertise.

The interview should give you a glimpse of the flesh-and-blood individual who is talking to you. Try to talk as little as

Sample Application Form

Name_____ Date_____
      (last)   (first)   (middle)

Address_____Phone no._____

Date of birth_____Height_____Weight_____

Place of birth_____U.S. citizen?_____

Social Security no._____No. of dependents_____

Health: Good_____Fair_____Poor_____

List handicaps, chronic ailments, serious illnesses:_____

_____

Person to notify in case of accident_____

Address_____Phone no._____

Minimum salary expected_____

Education

(name and address)	(from)	(to)	(graduated)
High School			
College			
Other			

Experience

(list last employer first)	(dates)	(job)	(reason for leaving)
Firm_____	From		
Address_____			
Supervisor_____	To		
Firm_____	From		
Address_____			
Supervisor_____	To		
Firm_____	From		
Address_____			
Supervisor_____	To		

possible. Listen instead. Your task is to control, to direct the interview—not dominate it. Learn about the applicant. You're not out to trip this person up or find fault; you're trying to analyze qualifications.

While you're gathering facts, you also should answer any questions the applicant has. Salary, benefits, job description—all of these have to be determined well in advance of the interview. In many cases, the franchisor supplies you with all the necessary information. However, you may want to supplement your understanding by determining how similar positions in your area are set up. The job description guides you here.

After the interview, you should have an idea of whom you want to hire. It's important that you evaluate each interview while it is still fresh in your mind. You're now ready to make your final selection. This can only be accomplished after you have narrowed the applicant group down to a select few.

The next step is to check the background of each applicant to see if he or she has provided you with an accurate background. This is important. A recent article in the *New York Times* claimed that deception in job applicants appears to be increasing—understandable in a time of recession. The frauds perpetrated range from simple lying about college credits to covering up a dishonest past.

When you find an applicant who appears to possess all the qualifications the job demands, check out his or her credentials—as carefully as possible. This could entail calling previous employers just to see if the applicant has not lied about previous places of employment. You should, at the very least, be able to confirm addresses and times. However, obtaining information about reasons for job termination can be difficult. Some employees have sued their former bosses for ruining their reputations and hurting their chances to obtain new jobs. However, dig as deep as you feel necessary. If you discover at any point that the applicant has misrepresented himself or herself, you had better think twice about hiring that particular person.

All of this might seem a bit tedious, but it is very important nonetheless. Your employees can make or break you. Good, contented employees are extremely valuable assets. Bad, lazy, discontented, or downright dishonest workers can be albatrosses around your neck.

Your final selection should be carefully weighed. Take everything you have learned into consideration. Include personal feelings. If you just don't like one of the applicants, and feel strongly that you would find it difficult to work with the person, you'd better admit it to yourself.

It also is important to keep in touch with the ones you haven't chosen. Your first selection might not accept the job or might not work out. If that happens, it's a good idea to have a second and third choice lined up.

With some luck and some hard work, you should be able to find an employee for almost any type of position in any franchised business. At present, jobs are scarce, so you probably will have no trouble discovering applicants. But you still want the best you can get.

Chapter 11
Managing Your Employees

The New Employee / Training Programs / How to Supervise / Delegating Authority / Supervisor Checklist / Problems in People Management / Working with Relatives

As OWNER of a franchise, you wear many hats: local businessperson, member of a large organization, buyer, salesperson, and so on. But none is more important than being a good people manager. As the previous chapter stressed, the people you work with are important to both you and your business. You can approach this job as a tyrant or as a responsible individual.

The franchisor ofter provides hiring guidelines, and sometimes the franchisor's representatives aid you in the initial hiring process. But you can't rely upon them forever, and ultimately you need to know as much as you can about managing your employees.

Your employees are a crucial part of your business. Depending on the type of your franchise, you will have differing requirements for your employees. The owner of a real estate agency needs a kind of person for realtor positions different from the worker that a restaurant owner needs for counter help.

But no matter what kind of business you set up, your employees are the people you work with day in and day out for, hopefully, a long time. If not, you may spend a great deal of money handling a high turnover of employees.

The New Employee

Perhaps the most difficult time for the new franchise owner is the first few months. This is another reason why good franchises are so attractive. You're not entirely left on your own; you have the experience and help of the franchisor to lean on. While you're learning the ropes, though, you also have to consider that the new employees are in the same position. Eventually you'll be in total charge of them and their actions, so it would be helpful if you took command as soon as possible.

Part of effective management relies on your ability to communicate your needs to the people who work with you. This communication is based upon the job description you have prepared or have obtained from your franchisor. You must give the employee strong, clear directions on the job. He or she must understand and be comfortable with the responsibilities.

It's also important to understand that your employees will act as individuals. Luckily, as owner and manager of a small business, you'll certainly get to know the people you work with day in day out. You'll probably discover that they can't be pushed into a single mold. You'll find that some employees have to be told exactly what to do, and others are motivated to take initiatives themselves. Both can be valued employees when treated right, but, on the other hand, when either type is managed poorly the business suffers.

Different Strokes for Different Workers

Herb, who worked as a car salesman, could be depended on to show up on time and do a fine job. Whenever he was told to handle a customer, do some extra paperwork, or supervise the maintenance crew, he cheerfully performed his job. The franchise owner could rely upon him to do almost anything—as long as he was given proper direction.

Dave, on the other hand, came in early, left late, and always had the job done before he was asked. Dave had that extra something that separates good employees from exemplary ones. Herb was a good employee, but Dave was the sort who could be trusted to run the shop—and he was eventually made an assistant manager. As manager, you have to be able to handle all types of employees—the Daves, the Herbs, and the marginal ones.

To help your new employees adjust to their jobs, you may have to institute a training program. The franchisor might initially help you set one up. The company can probably provide you with either a manual or instructors to help you train your employees. In some cases, a few hours or days are all that's necessary. In other instances, such as training a manager for your business, the instruction may last several weeks.

Training Programs

It may be helpful to you to establish your own training program on site when you've become settled in your franchise. The checklist from the SBA on pages 94–100 can help you plan your own training program.

The various types of training programs include:

- *Vestibule training.* Here, a job-like setting is created for the trainee to practice on before actually doing the real job.
- *Apprenticeship.* This process generally takes years. It is used to develop a trainee into a fully skilled craftsperson, such as a plumber or electrician.
- *Internship.* This type of training isn't just for doctors. In various fields, a business and a school cooperate in a program to provide students with practical business experience while they are still attending school.
- *Outside training.* Here, the employee is sent away to

a school, class, or seminar to learn specific skills he or she couldn't be taught at work.

- *On-the-job training.* This, of course, is the most popular method of training. The trainee simply learns the job while working at it.

Since there are so many different types of franchises, all these forms of training might apply at some point. Certainly, most of the training for the lower level positions has to be on the job. You can't afford to lose an employee to a long training programs located away from work. For higher level employees, such as assistant or night managers, the franchise organization may have training programs, such as courses for managers, that can be beneficial.

Checklist for Developing a Training Program

What Is the Goal of the Training?

The questions in this section are designed to help the owner-manager in defining the objective or goal to be achieved by a training program. Whether the objective is to conduct initial training, to provide for upgrading employees, or to retrain for changing job assignments, the goal should be spelled out before developing the plan for the training program.

	yes	*no*
1. Do you want to improve the performance of your employees?	□	□
2. Will you improve your employees by training them to perform their present tasks better?	□	□
3. Do you need to prepare employees for newly developed or modified jobs?	□	□
4. Is training needed to prepare employees for promotion?	□	□
5. Is the goal to reduce accidents and increase safety practices?	□	□
6. Should the goal be to improve employee attitudes, especially about waste and spoilage practices?	□	□
7. Do you need to improve the handling of materials in order to break production bottlenecks?	□	□
8. Is the goal to orient new employees to their jobs?	□	□

9. Will you need to teach new employees about   ☐   ☐
   overall operation?
10. Do you need to train employees so they can help   ☐   ☐
   teach new workers in an expansion program?

What Does the Employee Need to Learn?

Once the objective or goal of the program is set, you need to determine the subject matter. The following questions are designed to help you decide what the employee needs in terms of duties, responsibilities, and attitudes.

		yes	no
11.	Can the job be broken down into steps for training purposes?	☐	☐
12.	Are there standards of quality that trainees can be taught?		
13.	Are there certain skills and techniques that trainees must learn?	☐	☐
14.	Are there hazards and safety practices that must be taught?	☐	☐
15.	Have you established the methods that employees must use to avoid or minimize waste and spoilage?	☐	☐
16.	Are there materials-handling techniques that must be taught?	☐	☐
17.	Have you determined the best way for the trainees to operate the equipment?	☐	☐
18.	Are there performance standards that employees must meet?	☐	☐
19.	Are there attitudes that need improvement or modification?	☐	☐
20.	Will information on your products help employees to do a better job?	☐	☐
21.	Should the training include information about the location and use of tool cribs and so on?	☐	☐
22.	Will the employee need instruction about departments other than his own?	☐	☐

What Type of Training?

The type of training to be offered has an important bearing on the balance of the program. Some types lend themselves to achieving all of the objectives or goals, but others are limited. Therefore you should review the advantages of each type in relation to your objective or goal.

	yes	no
23. Can you train on-the-job so that employees can produce while they learn?	☐	☐
24. Shoul you have classroom training conducted by a paid instructor?	☐	☐
25. Will a combination of scheduled on-the-job training and vocational classroom instruction work best for you?	☐	☐
26. Can your goal be achieved with a combination of on-the-job training and correspondence courses?	☐	☐

What Method of Instruction?

One or more methods of instruction may be used. Some are better for one type of training than another: for example, lectures are good for imparting knowledge, and demonstrations are good for teaching skills.

	yes	no
27. Does the subject matter call for a lecture or series of lectures?	☐	☐
28. Should the instructor follow up with discussion sessions?	☐	☐
29. Does the subject matter lend itself to demonstrations?	☐	☐
30. Can operating problems be simulated in a classroom?	☐	☐
31. Can the instructor direct trainees while they perform the job?	☐	☐

What Audiovisual Aids Will You Use?

Audiovisual aids help the instructor to make his points and enable the trainees to grasp and retain the instructions.

	yes	no
32. Will a manual of instruction—including job instruction sheets—be used?	☐	☐
33. Will trainees be given an outline of the training program?	☐	☐

34. Can outside textbooks and other printed materials be used? □   □
35. If the training lends itself to the use of motion pictures, film strips, or slides, can you get ones that show the basic operation? □   □
36. Have you drawings or photographs of the machinery, equipment, or products that could be enlarged and used? □   □
37. Do you have miniatures or models of machinery and equipment that can be used to demonstrate the operation? □   □

What Physical Facilities Will You Need?

The type of training, the method of instruction, and the audiovisuals determine the physical facilities needed for the training. In turn, the necessary physical facilities determine the location of the training. For example, if a certain production machine is necessary, the training would be conducted in the shop.

	yes	no
38. If the training cannot be conducted on the production floor, do you have a conference room or a lunchroom in which it can be conducted?	□	□
39. Should the training be conducted off the premises, as in a nearby school, restaurant, hotel, or motel?	□	□
40. Will the instructor have the necessary tools, such as a blackboard, lectern, film projector, and a microphone (if needed)?	□	□
41. Will there be sufficient seating and writing surfaces (if needed) for the trainees?	□	□
42. If equipment is to be used, will each trainee be provided with his own?	□	□

What About the Timing?

The length of the training program will vary according to the needs of your company, the material to be learned, the ability of the instructor and the ability of the trainees to learn.

	yes	no
43. Should the training be conducted part-time and during working hours?	□	□
44. Should the sessions be held after working hours?	□	□
45. Will the instruction cover a predetermined period of time (for example, 4 weeks, 6 weeks, 3 months)?	□	□
46. Can the length of each session and the number of sessions per week be established?	□	□

Who Will Be Selected as Instructor?

The success of training depends to a great extent on the instructor. A qualified one could achieve good results even with limited resources. On the other hand, an untrained instructor may be unsuccessful even with the best program. You may want to use more than one person as instructor.

	yes	no
47. Can you fill in as an instructor?	□	□
48. Do you have a personnel manager who has the time and the ability to do the instructing?		
49. Can your foreman or department heads handle the instruction?	□	□
50. Should a skilled employee be used as the instructor?	□	□
51. Will you have to train the trainer, if he is an employee?	□	□
52. Is there is a qualified outside instructor available for employment on a part-time basis?		

Who Should Be Selected?

Employees should be selected for training on the basis of the goal of the program as well as their aptitudes, physical capabilities, previous experiences, and attitudes.

	yes	no
53. Should new employees be hired for training?	□	□
54. Should the training of new employees be a condition of employment?	□	□
55. Would you prefer trainees with previous experience in the work?	□	□
56. Are there present employees who need training?	□	□

	yes	no
57. Will you consider employees presently in lower-rated jobs who have the aptitude to learn?	☐	☐
58. Is the training to be a condition for promotion?	☐	☐
59. Will the training be made available to handicapped employees whose injury occurred while employed by the company?	☐	☐
60. Will employees be permitted to volunteer for the training?	☐	☐
61. Should employees displaced by job changes, departmental shutdowns, automation, and so on, be given the opportunity to be trained in other jobs?	☐	☐

What Will the Program Cost?

It may be desirable to compute the costs of your training before starting the program. Thus, you can budget sufficient funds for the program and use the budget as a tool for keeping training costs in line.

	yes	no
62. Should you charge the program for the space, the machines, and materials used?	☐	☐
63. Will the wages of trainees be included?	☐	☐
64. If the instructor is an employee, will his pay be included in the costs?	☐	☐
65. Will the time you and others spend in preparing and administering the program be part of the costs?	☐	☐
66. If usable production results from the sessions, should the results of it be deducted from cost of the program?	☐	☐

What Checks or Controls Will You Use?

The results of the training program need to be checked to determine the extent to which the original goal or objective was achieved.

	yes	no
67. Can you check the results of the training against the goal or objective?	☐	☐
68. Can standards of learning time be established against which to check the progress of the trainees?		
69. Can data on trainee performance be developed before, during and after training?	☐	☐

70. Will records be kept on the progress of each trainee? ☐ ☐
71. Will trainees be tested on the knowledge and skills acquired? ☐ ☐
72. Will the instructor rate each trainee during, and at the end of, the course? ☐ ☐
73. Will the trainee be followed up periodically by his foreman or department head to determine the long-range effects of his training? ☐ ☐
74. Should you personally check and control the program? ☐ ☐

How Should the Program Be Publicized?

Publicizing the company's training program in the community helps attract qualified job applicants. Publicity inside the company helps motivate employees to improve themselves.

	yes	no
75. If the program is announced to employees, will the announcement be made before the program starts? During the program?	☐	☐
76. Are pictures to be taken of the training sessions and used on bulletin boards and in local newspapers?	☐	☐
77. Should employees who complete the training be awarded certificates?	☐	☐
78. Should the certificates be presented at a special affair, such as a dinner?	☐	☐
79. When the certicates are awarded, will you invite the family of the trainees?	☐	☐
80. Should the local newspaper, radio, and TV people be invited to the "graduation" exercises?	☐	☐

How to Supervise

As the owner of the business, you wear even more hats—owner, manager, co-worker, employer, etc. As the owner of a franchise, you are responsible to others for maintaining a specific company image and paying royalties on time. Your job is to effectively wear all these hats at the same time.

It's not an easy job being different people at the same time. You can't afford to stand back and assume a distant management position. If you run a fastfood restaurant, you have to pitch in during rush hour and serve customers side by side with the people you hired. You'll probably have to clean up on occasion too.

Is it possible to be the boss of someone who sees you work at the same type of job they do? Of course it is, as long as you keep in command. You can't lose sight of the fact that the business ultimately depends upon you. Even though you occasionally work the counter, you also pay the bills and make most of the decisions that mean success or failure.

Your primary role as supervisor is to make sure that your employees perform as you want them to. There are basically three elements to the supervisor's job:

- If something is wrong, analyze the problem and correct it.
- If everything is running smoothly, find out why and keep up the good work.
- If everything is running smoothly, try to figure out how you can make it run even better.

As supervisor, you should share with your employees. This means letting them in on the inner workings of the business. Let them know why they are doing something. For example, it might help to share with them the reasons the franchisor demands things be done a certain way. Fastfood franchises often require their employees to wear standard uniforms. If the employees feel demeaned by this, explain that it is a proven method of maintaining a respected image. That approach works better than saying, "Wear the uniform or you're fired."

Delegating Authority

When your business grows too large for you to handle it alone, you should be prepared to delegate some of your authority. Your business is an entity that hopefully continues even if you aren't on hand every second to manage it. Some fast-food franchises are open 24 hours a day. Just try not delegating authority if you own that kind of business. You may last 2 days.

It's a matter of trust. The franchisor trusts you to own and operate a piece of the business he or she developed. And you have to learn to trust your employees to handle specific duties. You can't do it all.

It may take several weeks or even months to reach a point where you're comfortable with your help, but if you have hired the best people you could, taken advantage of all the help the franchisor offered, and set up a good training program, there should be no reason why you can't delegate responsibilities.

Ask yourself what would happen to your franchise if you were suddenly hospitalized for a month. Certainly, your franchisor may step in and help with a temporary manager, but that would cost you money. Could your employees work on their own? Could you trust them to hold the fort, or would your enterprise collapse without you there minding the store? If your business would collapse without you, you may need to restructure your organization.

Many people make the mistake of trying to run their businesses in their heads. They don't allow anyone else to get in on the the inner workings. A good manager shares all the steps of ordering, bookkeeping, and general management with an employee who can handle that aspect of the business. Your franchise organization is fine to lean upon, but they would prefer generally that you depend on your own resources.

Supervisor Checklist

It all boils down to some do's and don'ts. You should:
- Lead
- Provide an example

- Be understanding
- Motivate
- Delegate

You should not:

- Try to do everything
- Oversupervise
- Be inconsistent
- Be negative

Problems in People Management

Things won't always go smoothly for you as you continue to operate your business. You'll be bound to face a few hurdles as you manage your employees. And you can't expect the franchisor to shoulder every complaint. At this stage, they are your people, and you have to know how to handle them.

First, consider a few of the common difficulties that you may have to face in personnel management such as:

- Absenteeism
- Tardiness
- Incompetence
- Decline of effectiveness on the job
- Criminal behavior
- Criticizing employees
- Disciplining employees
- Firing

It's up to you to resolve such difficulties before they become serious by heading off the smaller problems before they develop further. For example, an employee who is often late must be dealt with before that lateness develops into chronic absenteeism.

Communications are very important. If an employee has taken too much personal time, sit down and get to the root of the problem. Let the employee know that you are con-cerned, but although you can commiserate over the prob-lem, you can't afford to shoulder it.

Don't save up grievances against one of your employees and months later haul them out for airing in front of the other employees. "Do it now" should be your motto.

If you discover that your employees are stealing merchandise, you should usually call the authorities immediately. Of course, you must evaluate any situation and take what seems the best step. Don't expose yourself to any danger, but don't allow a bad situation to get worse.

What do you do if you run a personnel agency and one of your employees takes home stationery supplies? The employee's defense will probably be that everyone else does it. If that's the case, you had better take a long, hard look, because you've got a serious problem. Petty pilferage can certainly add up. It may not be an outright dismissable offense, but you must institute rules so your business isn't slowly bled to death.

Disciplining can be very difficult in a small business. What you are doing is punishing an employee for breaking rules. Hopefully, in your dealings with employees, you'll be able to head off any disciplining with a long talk. If the behavior continues, if, for example, an employee is constantly tardy, you may have to dock his or her pay—which in turn leads to other strains.

If the situation just becomes not worth it, you may have to let the problem employee go. The main question you have to ask yourself is whether your action is justified. Are you being capricious or, in your best judgment, will keeping that employee hurt your business? If your action is justified, then you have no other choice. Again, this is the final step in a long process, but if there is nothing you can do to help this employee fit in, fire him or her.

The actual action of firing is messy at times. It's an emotional time bomb for both you and your employee. Because there is so much tension involved, your best approach is factual, straightforward, and unemotional. When you finally do fire an employee, have all the facts available, give your reasons, listen patiently, be firm, and, above all else, don't lose your temper and start a shouting match. In most cases your employee won't physically assault you, but you're tempting fate if you start screaming or engage in name calling.

Working with Relatives

Working side by side with a family member has its own rewards and its own drawbacks. One way to get around the problem of hiring employees and checking their background is to get a relative to work for you. Yet that same relative is going to have to learn to take orders from you and to work as if he or she had been hired off the street.

A great deal about working with relatives is positive. They often feel they have more of a stake in the business. If they are members of your immediate family—sons, daughters, mothers, fathers, husbands, wives—they probably are working for less money than would be paid to any other employee. Many businesses couldn't operate if relatives didn't pitch in.

Many small Chinese restaurants are family affairs. The owner may be the father, who doubles as a chef, alongside his wife and mother. The waiters may be sons and daughters and their spouses. And since the Chinese have an extended sense of family, there may also be aunts, uncles, nephews, and cousins galore.

It's worth noting that Chinese restaurants have an excellent record of survival. One reason is their owners' willingness to work very hard. Another reason is that many utilize the labor of relatives.

But, of course, problems come with working with relatives too. A son or daughter in the business may cause a certain amount of uneasiness among other employees. The boss's kids always get best treatment, the best jobs, and will ultimately run the business, so there's not much chance for nonrelatives to advance. It may not be fair, but it's often true. A parent may groom a child to take over the business—and this naturally causes some resentment among nonrelative employees. The only way around that problem is to be as fair as possible and to compensate all employees properly. Every one of your employees also must be made to feel a part of the business. Their morale must be kept as high as possible. They may not ever aspire to own the business one day, but they will be assured of good treatment.

Another problem is the unproductive relative. This one can be murderous. It's tough to fire a close relative, but sometimes that is exactly what you have to do. If the business is suffering, the choice will probably be pretty easy.

A related problem arises when an employee, say a rich aunt, lends you money to buy your franchise, with the stipulation that your nephew or niece be given a job. If the young person is any good, you may say fine and bless the deal. But if he or she has limited talents and no liking for work, you may want to reconsider the loan.

You also should carefully consider all the permutations of what accepting a relative as a silent partner means. Be sure that any dealings with money are handled as if your uncle or whoever were a complete stranger. Handshakes are not acceptable. Have a written agreement drawn up. You don't want your relative suddenly to demand the money back and leave you out in the cold.

A legal agreement is just as much for your relative's protection as well. The people they loan money to can (and do) forget to make payments—after all, they reckon, a mother or aunt wouldn't sue, would they? It is only fair to deal with your blood relatives as scrupulously as you would with any stranger.

There is no reason not to go into business with a relative as long as:

- You are compatible with each other.
- You communicate easily with each other.

- You all agree from the start about how the business will be run.
- Everyone's duties are well defined.
- Everyone understands that you are the boss.
- Everyone understands that the business comes first.

Chapter 12

Promoting Your Franchise Yourself

*The Franchise as a Community Business /
Publicity / Advertising*

ONE MAJOR REASON to purchase a franchise is that you are buying a well-known image. Often, this image has been created and enhanced by national advertising. That advertising, by the way, is not free; you pay for it either in your royalty check or as a specific cost. You can also do a lot yourself to help your own business. You yourself can draw attention in many ways to that business, not just the entire franchise.

This is called promotion or publicity. It can range from sponsoring local Little League teams to raising money for charities to celebrating business anniversaries. In many instances, the franchisor provides you with ways of promoting your business. However, you may come up with more germane ways of creating a rapport with your community.

Difficulties arise when your promotion or publicity does not conform with your franchise's image: McDonald's would look with little favor upon a restaurant that sponsored tag team female mud wrestling. Before you put into effect any plan that you have any question about, contact your franchise's representative. He or she will quickly tell you if your idea is acceptable.

The Franchise as a Community Business

Your franchise is not merely one among many shops; it is your business. Although you can't do just anything you want, you still can generate some more business and excitement by becoming a valued member of the community. As owner of a small business, you don't exist as an island in a sea of customers. You, whether you like it or not—and hopefully you like it—are a member of the community. You pay taxes, you vote, and you are also a consumer of other goods.

Therefore, you should strive to be a friend of your community. There are many ways you can hurt your business if you don't pay attention to the needs and sensitivities of your neighbors. For example, if you have a fast-food restaurant, you must have a good trash system. Many communities have been outraged by some restaurant's napkins and dirty paperwares blowing around the streets. In fact, any business must make an effort to keep the surroundings neat, clean, and unobtrusive.

Since you attract more customers with honey, be positive. Your franchisor probably stresses the old cliché, the customer is always right; but you and your employees can also project an image of helpfulness that goes a long way toward enhancing your reputation.

Publicity

Taking an active role in the community is a start. Next, you must tell that community all about your business. You can do this in several ways. One is by telling them straight out about your business and the products or services you sell; this involves advertising and is discussed a little later. The second way is by publicizing your business.

Publicity and advertising aren't the same. With advertising, you're paying the media to tell the public about you. You pay for space on a printed page or for an amount of time in a broadcast. With publicity, in a sense, the shoe is on the other foot. You are providing the media with information about your business that they can use as news.

There are different levels of publicity. A Hollywood star often has a staff of publicists looking for ways to get his or her name into the press or on the TV. As a business owner in a community, you're trying to find something, or create something, that will get your business's name in the paper or on local radio or television.

Tried and true methods include sponsoring a contest for athlete of the week or waiter or waitress of the week, and supporting local sports tournaments. Local businesses at least get their names in the paper when they sponsor any kind of sports team in recognized town or county leagues. Joe's Bar and Grill women's softball team will constantly be in the paper—especially if they win.

If you're ambitious, you may even be able to write a press release about an event connected with your business. Perhaps one of your employees has a special hobby or history—an ancestor may have come over on the ship after the Mayflower. A more mundane occurance might be the expansion of your business or the addition of something new that would interest editors.

Remember, when writing a release, keep it simple and direct. No editor likes to receive a release as long as *War and Peace*. Include all the facts and don't try to make it cute or exciting. A good litany to follow is the journalist's question routine—tell who, what, where, when, why, and how. Answer those questions in the release as clearly and concisely as possible.

Advertising

Franchises often can't rely just on the advertising campaign at a national level. Car dealerships, for example, do quite a bit of advertising on their own. Think how often you've seen an ad in the newspaper, listened to a radio commercial, or seen the dealer him or herself on a local television station. Your franchise also may help you with local advertising.

There are several methods of advertising. One or more of the following may be effective for your franchise:

Phone Books. Some franchisors require their franchisees to purchase space in both the white and yellow pages of the phone directory. They provide the franchisee with guidelines and approve all ads that go in the phone book.

The Yellow Pages are a fine place to advertise, and you may want to purchase space for a larger advertisement instead of settling for just a listing. Many people use the Yellow Pages to locate the right business, and a larger ad can attract their attention better. Take some time and check through your local Yellow Pages. Which ads catch your eye? Would a similar ad help your business?

If you have a local neighborhood directory, try to get space in that book as well. Chances are that most of your customers will be local residents.

Publications. This covers a wide variety of papers and magazines. Your local newspaper is an excellent source, but how about regional magazines? They may offer a way of both buying ads and obtaining some publicity.

Another source is the local high school or college paper or yearbook, where an ad at least buys you some good will. Who knows, ads in those publications may get you a few more customers. Generally the price is right.

One of the best types of publications for small businesses is a local flyer that is distributed in supermarkets or mailed free to residents. Don't underestimate these little papers as a method of drawing customers. With a little research, you'll probably discover that thousands of people in your neighborhood read one of them faithfully.

These are the major types of publications you will use. Check them carefully before you plunge in and buy a full-page ad. Find out what the rates are and see if they fall within your budget. Don't go overboard and plaster your franchise's name all over the county—more often isn't always better. You need to know your market and advertise with the nature of that particular market firmly in mind. If you want to reach a readership of young married couples, don't advertise in *Retirement Age*.

Radio/Television. Local radio also provides an affordable way for you to advertise. As with publications, however, you need to have some idea of who the audience is. A fast-food franchise may be well advertised on an all rock music station, but a lawn care business wouldn't get much of a response.

Television used to be far too expensive for all but the largest franchises—car dealerships, hotels, larger restaurants. But recently, there has been something of a revolution: it's cable TV, and it can be very inexpensive and reasonably effective. In its simplest form, a local cable channel might merely run the words of your ad on the bottom of the screen. Or you might tape a commercial—for a good deal more money, depending on the length of the spot. If you have a local cable channel, investigate—it may be a good investment.

Theaters/Billboards. In a sense, these methods of advertising are holdovers from a bygone era, before television. Yet billboards, especially, can be useful if you have a business that attracts motorists—a restaurant, camp ground, or hotel. On the other hand, paying for filmed advertising that precedes a movie has rather limited paybacks. However, if you own a fast-food restaurant in the same shopping mall as a theater, you may get a few customers with the right ad.

Being a good member of the community, managing publicity, and buying advertising all can help your business prosper. The two major things you need to do before you proceed is, first, to make sure you can afford the advertising, and second, to make sure that your activities in promoting your business meet with the approval of the franchisor.

Chapter 13

Bookkeeping

Types of Records

THE WHOLE POINT of your being in business is to make money. But no matter how much money you make, you can fritter away a substantial amount of it unless you keep accurate and up-to-date records. Your franchisor will certainly demand such records.

Usually the franchise organization provides you with sample books and trains you in the art of keeping them. Like the other chapters in this section, this one on bookkeeping is meant to supplement what they've taught you.

Good records are more than a task to hurry through at the end of each day. They are actually a fine business tool you can use productively. Your records can tell you how your business is doing; they can reveal trends; when you're doing well they can pinpoint what you did right; when you're doing poorly they can help you to discover why.

Essentially your records should answer the following questions from the SBA publication *Starting and Managing a Small Business of Your Own*:

- How much business am I doing?
- What are my expenses?
- What is my gross profit margin; my net profit?

- How much am I collecting on my charge business?
- What is the condition of my working capital?
- How much cash do I have on hand and in the bank?
- How much do I owe my suppliers?
- What is my net worth—the value of my ownership of the business?
- What are the trends in my receipts, expenses, profits, and net worth?
- Is my financial position improving or growing worse?
- How do my assets compare with what I owe? What is the percentage of return on my investment?
- How many cents out of each dollar of sales are net profit?

These and other questions can be answered after a review of your records. Your franchisor will also be interested in records that provide him or her with a solid picture of how your business is working out. To the franchisor, you're a piece of a large organization. The records you supply the franchise organization become a slice of data for their overall bookkeeping process.

Record keeping depends, logically enough, on your documenting all business-related transactions—purchases, sales, and expenses. You should jot down these transactions daily. It is vital to your business that everything be accounted for. You have to have adequate records to satisfy not only your franchisor, but also the federal, state, and local governments for tax purposes; banks or other sources of money if you ever decide to take out a loan; and any prospective purchaser who wants an accurate picture of your business if you decide to sell.

Types of Records

The types of records you need to keep depend on the type of business you're in. If you're large enough, you may even benefit from installing computerized bookkeeping. Even if you're relatively small, there is a wide variety of computers and computer programs now on the market that you might find helpful in your business. But a computer can't do all the work by itself. You have to supply it with all of the information. In the beginning, you should keep a duplicate set of books until you are sure that your computer is operating properly and that you or your operators know enough about the operation of the system so that you won't lose records by inadvertantly shutting off power or accidentally dumping information.

Your franchisor will certainly let you know what kind of records are needed to support your business. The following list shows many of the records your business may need (from SBA):

Inventory and Purchasing. These records provide facts to help with buying and selling.

> Inventory control record
> Item perpetual inventory record
> Model stock plan
> Out-of-stock sheet
> Open-to-buy record
> Purchase order file
> Open purchase order file
> Supplier file
> Returned goods file
> Price change book
> Accounts payable ledger

Sales records. These records reveal facts to determine sales trends.

> Record of individual sales transactions
> Summary of daily sales
> Sales plan
> Sales promotion plan

Cash Records. These records show what is happening to cash.

Daily cash reconciliation
Cash receipts journal
Cash disbursements journal
Bank reconciliation

Credit. These records keep track of who owes you and whether they are paying on time.

Charge account application
Accounts receivable ledger
Accounts receivable aging list

Employees. These records maintain information that is legally required and also is helpful for efficient management of personnel.

Record of employee earnings and amounts withheld
Employee's withholding exemption certificate (Form W–4)
Record of hours worked
Record of expense allowances
Employment applications
Record of changes in rate of pay
Record of reasons for termination of employment
Record of employee benefits
Job descriptions
Crucial incidents record

Fixtures and Property. These records keep facts needed for taking depreciation allowances and for insurance coverage and claims.

Equipment record
Insurance register

Bookkeeping. These records, in addition to some of the above, are needed if you use a double-entry bookkeeping system.

General journal
General ledger

Don't be shocked by the number and variety of records that could be kept. You don't have to keep all of them, and only a few require daily entries. Those that don't should be stored in a secure place, such as a safety deposit box.

The primary records you'll probably keep are the following: a daily record or journal, a ledger, a profit and loss statement, a balance sheet, and a checkbook.

Daily Journal and Ledger. This, as mentioned before, is simply a record of your daily transactions. There are essentially two sections or two books: one for cash receipts, the other for cash disbursement. Simply put, the cash receipt book should detail all the information about your daily revenue from all sources. The cash disbursement book should detail every cent you had to pay for that day.

The raw material you gather in your journal is itemized, usually monthly, in another book, the ledger. The ledger sheets have their own headings—payroll, purchases, sales, and so on. And they provide you with your basic business facts for that month.

Profit and Loss Statement. A profit and loss statement is a useful business tool that simply states how much money your business made or lost. You use the amounts written down in your ledger as the source material. The profit and loss statement should be redone every 3 months so you have a good idea of the trends in your business.

Balance Sheet. The profit and loss statement is an excellent source for determining cash flow and costs, but to determine how much your business is actually worth, you need a balance sheet. Essentially, the balance sheet is a summation of the ledger. It lists your total assets and liabilities and includes property values, depreciation, inventories, and the rest of what you have tied up in the business. It also includes everything you owe, such as outstanding loans.

Checkbook. Your checkbook is another important tool. Handled properly, it can provide you with an important backup source of information for such people as IRS investigators. Handled improperly it can drain the dollars away.

The rules about maintaining a checking account are quite simple. First, keep accurate and complete check stubs for every transaction. This is vital: you can't trust your memory. Second, don't mix up personal and business checking accounts. Open a separate account for each kind of use. This is important for tax purposes. Who's to say what is for business and what is for personal use if there is only a single checking account? Third, try not to make out checks to cash for business purposes. You need the records; such checks can be cashed by anyone; and they might not be allowed as business deductions by the IRS.

If you're totally inexperienced in bookkeeping procedures, you will need to lean on two people. First, your franchisor: bookkeeping is as important to him or her as is it is to you. Second, your accountant: perhaps the same accountant who helped you select your franchise can give you additional help in selecting the best record system for you. Your accountant will almost certainly be a major source of all sorts of financial information; you'll probably maintain a reasonably close relationship with him or her, since you'll also need an accountant to prepare your taxes.

Part III
Franchise Work Section

THIS SECTION is set up to help you:

- Start your franchise research
- Compare different franchise data
- Find other sources of franchise information

This section presents another checklist put out by the government to help you compare the franchises you're interested in. It also lists the names, addresses, and basic information for many current franchisors as of early 1980.

The list is taken from the *Franchise Opportunities Handbook* (United States Department of Commerce), which contains a comprehensive list of franchised businesses.

Checklist for Evaluating a Franchise

The Franchise

1. Did your lawyer approve the franchise contract you are considering after he studied it paragraph by paragraph?
2. Does the franchise call upon you to take any steps that are, according to your lawyer, unwise or illegal in your state, county, or city?
3. Does the franchise give you an exclusive territory for the length of the franchise or can the franchisor sell a second or third franchise in your territory?
4. Is the franchisor connected in any way with any other franchise company handling similar merchandise or services?
5. If the answer to the last question is yes, what is your protection against this second franchisor organization?
6. Under what circumstances can you terminate the franchise contract and at what cost to you, if you decide for any reason at all that you wish to cancel it?
7. If you sell your franchise, will you be compensated for your good will or will the good will you have built into the business be lost by you?

The Franchisor

8. How many years has the firm offering you a franchise been in operation?
9. Has it a reputation for honesty and fair dealing among the local firms holding its franchise?
10. Has the franchisor shown you any certified figures indicating exact net profits of one or more going firms which you personally checked yourself with the franchisee?
11. Will the firm assist you with:
    a. A management training program?
    b. An employee training program?
    c. A public relations program?
    d. Capital?
    e. Credit?
    f. Merchandising ideas?
12. Will the firm help you find a good location for your new business?
13. Is the franchising firm adequately financed so that it can carry out its stated plan of financial assistance and expansion?
14. Is the franchisor a one-man company or a corporation with an experienced management trained in depth (so that there would always be an experienced man at its head)?
15. Exactly what can the franchisor do for you that you cannot do for yourself?

16. Has the franchisor investigated you carefully enough to assure itself that you can successfully operate one of their franchises at a profit both to them and to you?
17. Does your state have a law regulating the sale of franchises and has the franchisor complied with that law?

You—The Franchisee

18. How much equity capital will you have to have to purchase the franchise and operate it until your income equals your expenses? Where are you going to get it?
19. Are you prepared to give up some independence of action to secure the advantages offered by the franchise?
20. Do *you* really believe you have the innate ability, training, and experience to work smoothly and profitably with the franchisor, your employees, and your customers?
21. Are you ready to spend much or all of the remainder of your business life with this franchisor, offering his product or service to your public?

Your Market

22. Have you made any study to determine whether the product or service that you propose to sell under franchise has a market in your territory at the prices you will have to charge?
23. Will the population in the territory given you increase, remain static, or decrease over the next 5 years?
24. Will the product or service you are considering be in greater demand, about the same, or less demand 5 years from now than today?
25. What competition exists in your territory already for the product or service you contemplate selling?
    a. Nonfranchise firms?
    b. Franchise firms?

You will find it useful to refer back to the checklist and worksheet that are presented on pages 58–73.

Current Franchisors

Automotive Products/Services

AAMCO TRANSMISSIONS, INC.
408 East Fourth Street
Bridgeport, Pennsylvania 19405
Dave Levy, Director of Franchise Sales

Description of operation: AAMCO centers repair, recondition, and rebuild transmissions for all cars. This is done by specially trained mechanics. Franchisees do not need to have a technical background, but should have a strong business background.

Number of franchisees: 834 in 50 states and across Canada

In business since: 1958

Equity capital needed: $35,000

Financial assistance available: A total investment of $85,000 required to open an AAMCO center in a major market. A total of $75,000 is required in a secondary market. Company can arrange financing for half of total requirement, if franchisee has good credit references. Franchisee has the option to arrange own outside financing.

Training provided: A comprehensive 6-week training course is provided at the company headquarters. In addition field training is provided at the opening of the operation to see that franchisee is properly launched.

Managerial assistance available: A consulting and operation division continually works with each center on a weekly basis to insure proper day-by-day operation. Monthly area meetings are held.

ABC MOBILE BRAKE
181 Wells Avenue
Newton Centre, Massachusetts 02159
David B. Slater, President
Ron Kopack, Executive Vice President

Description of operation: Franchisee operates customized Ford van outfitted with Ammco brake machining equipment, extensive parts inventory, and radio/telephone communications equipment, providing wholesale brake repair services to service stations and automotive repair shops nationwide. Franchisees do not need a technical background, but should be strongly motivated to achieve success through owning their own business.

Number of franchisees: 135 in 40 states

In business since: 1962

Equity capital needed: $10,500

Financial assistance available: Total investment of $31,700. Company can provide financing up to $21,200 to qualified applicants, or applicant can secure own financing.

Training provided: Comprehensive technical and sales training provided in Chicago followed by field training at opening of operation.

Managerial assistance available: Continuous managerial and technical assistance provided throughout term of franchise. Clinics, national conventions, national advertising, and merchandising programs and technical bulletins, as well as a monthly news magazine, bookkeeping system, and operations manual provide professional support to the business owner.

ABT SERVICE CENTERS
DIVISION OF ABT SERVICE CORPORATION
2339 South 2700 West
Salt Lake City, Utah 84119
William D. Platka, Director of Marketing & Real Estate

Description of operation: Alignment, brakes, tune-up repair centers that specialize in 1-day, high profit automobile, and truck service needs. Guaranteed, fast, economical service performed in a "new" 8 bay facility, with the "right" equipment and the "right" training, is the backbone of this franchise. A strong managerial background is essential; training will provide the rest.

Number of franchisees: 8 in 2 states

In business since: 1977

Equity capital needed: $51,000 (includes $10,000 operating capital)

Financial assistance available: Franchise includes 8 bay facility, signs, equipment, training with no need for additional equipment. Should a franchisee want additional equipment, financing through leasing companies, banks, and ABT is available to qualified applicants. Franchisee must be financially qualified to guarantee construction.

Training provided: 2 weeks will be spent in an ABT Service Center and at the company headquarters in Salt Lake City, Utah. This schedule will be increased if necessary. ABT operational people will then shift to franchisee's center for the training of his manpower. A grand opening will be prepared and held during this period.

Managerial assistance available: On a regular basis ABT personnel visit the franchisee to provide consultation in day-to-day operations and to analyze monthly progress. ABT provides operation manuals, training manuals, bookkeeping systems, insurance programs, advertising assistance, and other management tools.

ACC-U-TUNE
2510 Old Middle Field Way
Mountain View, California 94043
Stanley Shore, President

Description of operation: ACC-U-TUNE centers specialize in automotive tune-ups, lubrication and oil changes, air conditioning service, and other minor repair and auto maintenance services. Typical tune-up and complete lube, oil and filter change is less than $55, is done in about 1 hour while customer waits, and guaranteed in writing for 6,000 miles. Prices include both parts and labor.

Number of franchisees: 3 in California

In business since: 1975

Equity capital needed: $30,000 and excellent credit

Financial assistance available: Franchisee must have minimum of $30,000 in cash; financial assistance is available.

Training provided: Extensive preopening home-study course, classroom training (about 2 weeks), and 2 weeks on-the-job training. Training includes technical aspects of doing a tune-up, fundamentals of auto repair, bookkeeping, marketing, customer relations, shop maintenance.

Managerial assistance available: Complete technical manuals, advertising manuals, and operations manuals covering all day-to-day aspects of managing a profitable tune-up center.

AID AUTO STORES, INC.
1150 Metropolitan Avenue
Brooklyn, New York 11237
Alan Koller, National Sales Manager

Description of operation: Retail sales of automotive parts, tools, and accessories.

Number of franchisees: 78 in New York, New Jersey, Connecticut, and Florida

In business since: 1954

Equity capital needed: $40,000

Financial assistance available: None

Training provided: 30-day minimum. Continual assistance after initial training.

Managerial assistance available: All necessary to properly train franchisee to maintain a stable business.

DIAMOND QUALITY TRANSMISSIONS CENTERS OF AMERICA, INC.
P.O. Box 6147
Philadelphia, Pennsylvania 19115
Alfred Gold, President

Description of operation: Diamond Quality Transmissions Centers adjust, repair, service, recondition, and remanufacture automatic transmissions and 3- and 4-speed stick transmissions for cars and light trucks. Franchisee needs no previous automotive experience to be trained to manage a transmission center, no matter what occupation or profession previously held.

Number of franchisees: 4 in Pennsylvania and New Jersey

In business since: 1949

Equity capital needed: $10,000 to $35,000

Financial assistance available: Financing up to $20,000 to franchisees with good credit rating.

Training provided: 4 weeks training in salesmanship, management, and technical operations, which includes on-the-location training and promotion to assure a successful operation, will be provided.

Managerial assistance available: Simplified bookkeeping system available on a daily, weekly, or monthly basis. Service manuals and technical manuals are available. Seminars in operating technique and management salesmanship are available. On-the-location help available when requested to increase promotion and sales on a retail or wholesale basis.

DRIVE LINE SERVICE, INC.
P.O. Box 782
1309 Tradewind Circle
West Sacramento, California 95691
L. D. Wilson, President

Description of operation: Franchising specialized automotive service shops that perform complete drive shaft service, repair, remanufacture, modification, and balancing. Service Centers are based upon use of equipment and methods specifically designed to precisely work on all sizes and types of drive shafts.

Number of franchisees: 39 (plus 3 company-owned) in 17 states

In business since: 1971

Equity capital needed: Approximately $50,000 for equipment and franchise, plus $30,000 for operation capital

Financial assistance available: No financial assistance is currently offered.

Training provided: The franchise includes 2 weeks training for the franchisee and one other person. All expenses except living and travel are borne by franchisor. Training is conducted at the West Sacramento, California shop location or in one of several midwestern locations.

Managerial assistance available: Franchisor maintains a staff qualified to provide assistance over the duration of the franchise agreement in all matters of management, technical, and promotional. Unusual problems and solutions are passed throughout the organization by regularly scheduled communications, monthly newsletters, and unscheduled conferences.

NICK'S SYSTEMS INC.
DR. NICK'S TRANSMISSIONS INC.
150 Broad Hollow Road—Suite 300
Melville, New York 11747
Russ Bartolotta, Marketing Director

Description of operation: Transmission Service Centers providing quality repairs to all types of auto and light duty commercial vehicles in both the retail and wholesale trade.

Number of franchisees: 9 in New York

In business since: 1972; franchising since 1977

Equity capital needed: Up to $54,000. $10,500 franchise fee, $5,000 working capital required; remainder depending on inventory, lease equipment available, leasehold improvements necessary, and personal credit rating.

Financial assistance available: Financial advice and counseling is available when necessary and upon request. The prospective franchisee is responsible for an investment to cover initial licensing fees and operating capital.

Training provided: A comprehensive home office training program into all phases necessary to operate successfully your transmissions center. Also continuous field support and counseling.

Managerial assistance available: Prospective franchisee need not have any automotive technical experience. We provide on-going training and assistance in all phases of center operations, including but not restricted to center management, personnel selection and financial management. A professional co-op advertising program. Site selection assistance. Regular monthly meetings.

EAST COAST RADIATOR FRANCHISES, INC.
125 Lincoln Highway
Fairless Hills, Pennsylvania 19030
Richard D. Barton, Secretary Treasurer

Description of operation: Sales and service of complete radiator, heating, air conditioning, and cooling systems in automobiles and trucks.

Number of franchisees: 6 units in Pennsylvania

In business since: 1974

Equity capital needed: $29,975 (plus leasehold improvements and working capital)

Financial assistance available: If prospect has adequate down payment and enough equity, ECRF, Inc., will help prospect secure loan by going to lending institution with him.

Training provided: 3-week training course with complete technical, sales, and management covered. Training at company facility in Philadelphia, Pennsylvania. Travel and lodging not paid by ECRF, Inc.

Managerial assistance available: ECRF, Inc., provides on-going assistance through 2-week open period, and then weekly visits, periodic company meetings with other franchisees. Complete operations manual, continued advertising, and on-going business evaluation are also provided.

ECONO LUBE N' TUNE, INC.
18092 Skypark South
Suite A
Irvine, California 92714
Al Savage

Description of operation: A complete "turn-key" lubrication and tune-up shop.

Number of franchisees: 41 in California

In business since: 1973

Equity capital needed: Approximately $58,000

Financial assistance available: Total package approximately $78,000

Training provided: 1-month training in all phases of operation. We hire and train all employees.

Managerial assistance available: Day-to-day managerial and technical assistance is provided.

ENDRUST
1725 Washington Road
Suite 202
Pittsburgh, Pennsylvania 15241
William A. Griser, President

Description of operation: Engaged in establishing dealerships for automotive rustproofing. Dealers being owners and operators of body shops, new and used car dealers, tire dealers, gasoline service stations, and separate rustproofing centers.

Number of franchisees: 55 in 8 states

In business since: 1969

Equity capital needed: $25,000

Financial assistance available: None

Training provided: Company training in all phases of operation.

Managerial assistance available: All that is required by dealer.

E.P.I. INC.
P.O. Box 702
Summit, New Jersey 07901
W. C. Koppel, President

Description of operation: Manufacturers of world famous "Sparky, Washmobile" car wash equipment. *Sparky,* portable self-service coin-operated "50 cents, 75 cents and $1.00" car wash and wax systems. Also washes trucks, vans, campers, boats, etc. Washes with cold water. *Washmobile* "countdown" has a functional stainless steel housing, completely automatic, and consists of motors, gear boxes, air cylinders, industrial brushes, electric controls to run machine automatically, all copper piping, with automatic detergent system and detergent, and wax tanks and gauges. Optional: window brushes, 20 H.P. high velocity dryer, wheel washer, spray wax system, truck and guide, hose and trolley assembly, power pump, hot water heater, coin meter, vacuum cleaner, signs, towel dispenser, and waste receptacles.

Number of franchisees: 141 in 11 states and throughout the world

In business since: 1948

Equity capital needed: $35,900

Financial assistance available: Depending upon personal statements of applicants

Training provided: Company training in all phases of operation including merchandising and marketing programs and direction.

Managerial assistance available: As above plus marketing sales manager and factory engineers available for sales and technical experience as requested. This is available for as long as owner or franchisee has equipment and is without default.

THE FIRESTONE TIRE & RUBBER COMPANY
1200 Firestone Parkway
Akron, Ohio 44317
W. F. Tierney, Wholesale Sales Manager

Description of operation: Complete business franchise includes all phases for selling tires, auto and home supplies, and automotive services, backed up with national and local television, radio and newspaper advertising, periodic retail sales plans, display material, and many other sales and merchandising plans for increased sales and profits.

Number of franchisees: Over 14,000 direct including many more associate dealers operating throughout the U.S. and Canada

In business since: 1900

Equity capital needed: $50,000 or more; varies as to locations, business, equipment, and inventory

Financial assistance available: Sales and credit personnel counsel and assist franchisee to obtain necessary assistance through local sources or through company's assistance programs.

Training provided: Home office and field personnel are available at all times to train the dealer and his employees in all phases of sales and business management. This continuous program helps to insure an efficient and successful operation. Films, self-training programs, on-the-job training programs, etc., are constantly being revised and up-dated to keep dealer informed on all aspects of his business.

Managerial assistance available: Home office and local sales personnel are available to give assistance on any matter requested, including all phases of retail selling.

FRANK'S MUFFLER SHOPS
Division of FRANK'S HOME & AUTO SUPPLY CO., INC.
P.O. Box 409
Delavan, Wisconsin 53115
Robert Hoppa, General Manager

Description of operation: Privately owned, fully integrated shops for installation of guaranteed automobile mufflers and shock absorbers on the most efficient, cost competitive basis.

Number of franchisees: 11 shops in Wisconsin

In business since: Franchising—1978, muffler shops—1969

Equity capital needed: $22,250

Financial assistance available: $40,000 needed to open average shop. Existing, operating shops up to $65,000. Franchisee will be counseled and assisted in setting up a plan and securing needed financing and leads. This is subject to credit rating of candidate.

Training provided: A complete training program on the technical aspects of operations is provided for the owner and the initial employees at the company master shop in Delavan, Wisconsin. This program will be supplemented by scheduled visits from technically oriented management personnel, and updating correspondence to individual shops.

Managerial assistance available: A qualified staff person will be available to train and assist in general business matters. This will cover all operational business affairs including customer contact, sales promotion, financial ratios, employee recruiting, wage structure, inventory levels, etc. Standardized bookkeeping procedures, forms, policies will be given under the overall franchising plan.

MAD HATTER MUFFLERS, INC.
7110 North 35th Avenue
Phoenix, Arizona 85021
Jay McKinley

Description of operation: Mad Hatter Mufflers of Florida, Inc., has devised a unique and uniform method for the sale and installation of automotive mufflers and exhaust system parts, in a free-standing muffler service center.

Number of franchisees: 40 in 20 states

In business since: 1976

Equity capital needed: Total package price $38,000

Financial assistance available: A total investment of $38,000 is necessary to open a Mad Hatter Muffler Center franchise. The down payment of $9,500 is needed, the balance plus $7,000 working capital.

Training provided: Intensive 7-day training course at the National Training Center in Largo, Florida. A minimum of 3 days at the franchisee's outlet under the supervision of a full-time Mad Hatter Trainer.

Managerial assistance available: Mad Hatter Mufflers of Florida, Inc., provides continual management and training services for the life of the franchise in such areas as advertising, new products, complete product and operational manuals, all forms, letterheads, envelopes, and point of sale material. Regional training directors are available in all areas to work closely with franchisees and visit the Mad Hatter Muffler Centers regularly to assist in solving problems and updating installation procedures, introducing new products, and training on same. Mad Hatter Mufflers sponsors meetings of franchisees and conducts marketing and product research to maintain high continued consumer acceptance.

MALCO PRODUCTS, INC.
361 Fairview Avenue
P.O. Box 892
Barberton, Ohio 44203
J. Ginley

Description of operation: Distributorship to sell complete line of automotive chemical specialities including cleaners, oil additives, brake fluid, etc., to service stations, garages, new and used car dealers, and industrial outlets. He is assigned a territory that can support him. The distributor and his men travel the area using step vans, selling to the above accounts.

Number of franchisees: 435 throughout the United States

In business since: 1953

Equity capital needed: $3,000 for inventory and investment only

Financial assistance available: None

Training provided: Thorough field and product training in the distributor's area by regional sales manager. Periodically during the year the regional sales manager spends time with the distributor and salesmen for training both in product knowledge and field training.

Managerial assistance available: Distributor sales meetings are held twice a year for further training. Complete managerial assistance provided through company personnel and field representatives.

MECHANICAL MAN CAR WASH FACTORY, INC.
6 Watson Place
Utica, New York 13502
Raymond Seakan, President

Description of operation: Manufacturing of self-service units, roll-over brush units with or without blowers, conveyors all sizes, self-contained mobile truck wash units, tractor trailer brush units, subway and train brush units, and any custom designed car wash unit.

Number of franchisees: 1,076 in 47 states

In business since: 1964

Equity capital needed: $16,500 to $62,000

Financial assistance available: 25 percent down payment, balance on bank loan or lease arrangement. Franchisee must have good credit references. No experience necessary. Franchisee has the option to arrange his own financing.

Training provided: A comprehensive training course at our factory on hiring labor, business management, operating car wash equipment, preventative maintenance, service, advertising, and promotion. Also, 1 week of assistance and training at the installation when it opens.

Managerial assistance available: We offer assistance in advertising, promotion, retraining of new personnel at our factory, telephone assistance daily, if necessary, along with meetings setup for new programs and expansion. Bimonthly letters sent with new ideas and promotions to help franchisee increase success.

MEINEKE DISCOUNT MUFFLER SHOPS, INC.
6330 West Loop South
Suite 103
Bellaire, Texas 77401
Harold Nedell, President

Description of operation: Meineke Discount Muffler Shops, Inc., offer fast, courteous service in the merchandising of automotive exhaust systems and shock absorbers. Unique inventory control and group purchasing power enable Meineke dealers to adhere to a "discount concept." No mechanical skills required.

Number of franchisees: 189 in 24 states

In business since: 1972

Equity capital needed: $58,337 investment for inventory, equipment, signs, furniture, fixtures, estimated lease, utility deposits, start-up costs, and working capital

Financial assistance available: Up $22,444 to qualified applicants.

Training provided: 3 weeks schooling and on-the-job training at Houston headquarters. In addition, Meineke provides continuous field supervision and group operational meetings.

Managerial assistance available: Meineke Discount Muffler operations manual provides clear and concise reference for every phase of the business. Home office staff analysis of weekly reports is provided on a continuous basis.

MIDAS-INTERNATIONAL CORP.
222 South Riverside Plaza
Chicago, Illinois 60606
William Strahan, Vice President

Description of operation: Automotive exhaust system, brake, shock absorbers, and front end alignment. Shops offer fast service "while you watch" in clean, pleasant, modern surroundings.

Number of franchisees: 1,200 in 50 states, Canada, and Puerto Rico

In business since: 1956

Equity capital needed: $125,000 investment for inventory, equipment, sign, furniture, fixtures, fees, and working capital

Financial assistance available: Franchise receives complete assistance in obtaining necessary financing from appropriate lending agencies with which Midas has working arrangements.

SPEEDI-LUBE, INC.
2500 N.E. 49th
Seattle, Washington 98105
Clayton N. Loges, Vice President

Description of operation: 10-minute oil change, lubrication, and filter replacement performed by professional technicians in conveniently located and comfortable facilities.

Number of franchisees: 11 in Washington

In business since: 1977

Equity capital needed: $40,000

Financial assistance available: No direct financing provided, however, assistance will be rendered with franchisee's application for outside sources of capital.

Training provided: Formal classroom and on-site training provided over 3-week period. Additional training available at franchisee's request.

Managerial assistance available: Speedi-Lube provides technical and operational manuals with regular updates, construction support, business forms, operational control systems, accounting programs, sales, advertising, and marketing programs.

SPEEDY TRANSMISSION CENTERS, INC.
50 Don Park Road, Unit 1
Markham, Ontario
Canada L3R 1J3
William A. Gibson

Description of operation: Speedy Transmission Centers repair, rebuild, and recondition automatic and standard transmission for automobiles and trucks. Franchisees do not require a mechanical background. Trained mechanics are used for the technical aspect of the operation. A franchisee should have some business management experience.

Number of franchisees: 30 in California, Texas, Florida, New York, and West Virginia; Canadian associated—90

In business since: Established in Canada as a franchisor in 1963, in the United States in 1973

Equity capital needed: Total investment $50,000

Financial assistance available: Financial packages are available to qualified franchisees through various suppliers of the franchisor. Both financing and leasing is available in most areas. Franchisor will assist applicant in preparing and presenting a financial plan to secure financing.

Training provided: Prior to opening the franchisor provides a 2-week course covering sales, management systems, advertising, accounting, and operations management in addition to 2 weeks on-the-job training.

Managerial assistance available: The franchisor assists in securing a location, building design and layout, initial equipment and stock ordering, preopening and postopening operations and management supervision by the operations department. Continued periodical operations support, advertising promotions, and technical support is supplied on an "on-going basis."

STOP A FLAT—CHALFONT INDUSTRIES
608 Masons Mill Business Park
Huntingdon Valley, Pennsylvania 19006
M. L. Stein

Description of operation: Auto after market chemicals to be applied to automobiles for consumer protection and safety. Also sells other car-care chemicals to be used on all new and used cars.

Number of franchisees: 65 in 41 states and worldwide

In business since: 1976

Equity capital needed: $12,500 to $100,000

Financial assistance available: Some financing available.

Training provided: Initial 2-week training plus constant field training.

Managerial assistance available: Constant field and telephone contact.

THRIFT-WAY AUTO CENTERS INC.
396 Union Boulevard
Totowa, New Jersey 07512
Robert Bozzagtra, President

Description of operation: Four bay and up automotive centers that specialize in brake, front-end, shocks, alignments, muffler, tune-up, and oil change. All work performed by specially trained mechanics. Operator does not need previous automotive experience.

Number of franchisees: 20 in New Jersey and New York

In business since: 1977

Equity capital needed: $18,000 plus building lease securities

Financial assistance available: A total investment is $49,900, which, excluding working capital, is required. We assist in securing financing on the balance of investment, which is $31,000.

Training provided: 6 weeks of intensive training in company shop is provided. In addition, Thrift-Way provides continuous field supervision.

Managerial assistance available: Company representative will assist during opening of new shop. There is continued managerial, technical, and advertising assistance at all times during the time of the franchise.

TIDY CAR INC.
3918 Broadway
Cheektowaga, New York 14227
Gary Goranson, President

Description of operation: Tidy Car Inc., offers a unique "mobile appearance maintenance service" that is performed by independent operators (franchisees) for the owners of cars, vans, marinecraft, aircraft, RVs and other vehicles. Weather permitting, the service can be performed almost anywhere the customer's vehicle is parked, at his home or office, days, evenings, or weekends. Services include exterior, long-term protective shine on painted surfaces; vinyl roof reconditioning; interior detailing; and a fabric protection process to prevent permanent staining from spots and spills.

Number of franchisees: More than 2,000 in all 50 states, Canada, Puerto Rico, Trinidad, Curacao, Philippines, Malaysia, Australia, Guam, Tahiti, Thailand, Hong Kong, Germany, Holland, Belgium, Norway, England, Japan, Kuwait, Israel, Virgin Islands, and other countries around the globe

In business since: 1976

Equity capital needed: Approximately $1,500

Financial assistance available: A total investment of approximately $1,500 is necessary to commence business on a part-time basis. This investment is for inventory of equipment, materials, supplies, and advertising material. There is no initial franchise fee as such; however an on-going royalty payment of $2 per job (minimum: $20 per month) is payable. No financing arrangements are offered due to the small required investment.

Training provided: No formal training program is required. Franchisee is furnished with a comprehensive 115-page operator's manual and can gain required experience doing his/her family car(s). Further, it is recommended that a new franchisee gain experience doing friends' and relatives' vehicles before commencing to solicit the public. Any questions which the franchisee may have relating to any information not contained in the operator's manual are handled via mail and/or telephone from the head office.

Managerial assistance available: Tidy Car Inc., provides continuing assistance and information to its franchisees through its monthly publication "TIDYings From Tidy Car." In addition, Tidy Car Inc., sponsors regional meetings throughout the United States and Canada from time to time that include workshop sessions to answer technical and administrative areas of the business. Tidy Car Inc. also provides franchisees with advertising materials and suggestions including newspaper repros, display kit (car dealer showrooms, mail displays, car shows, etc.), advertising brochures, and other promotional aids and guidelines. Tidy Car Inc. also provides assistance and consultation by telephone and letter when requested. Complete guidelines are presented in all phases of the operation including application, recruiting workers, advertising and promotion, record keeping, etc.

Auto/Trailer Rentals

AJAX RENT A CAR COMPANY
8816 West Olympic Boulevard
Beverly Hills, California 90211
Jerry Kenney, Director, Ajax System

Description of operation: Automobile and truck rental.

Number of franchisees: Over 100 coast to coast

In business since: 1969

Equity capital needed: From $25,000 to $100,000, depending on size of territory

Financial assistance available: None

Training provided: 2 weeks at the system's headquarters. Complete procedure manual provided, which is updated at all times by the head office.

Managerial assistance available: Accounting assistance available as well as continuous guidance regarding the acquisition and disposition of fleets. Periodic visits from district manager to keep franchisee aware of new developments in the industry. National advertising and free reservation system.

AMERICAN INTERNATIONAL RENT-A-CAR
4241 Sigma Road
Dallas, Texas 75240
William E. Lobeck, Jr., General Manager

Description of operation: Franchisor of daily car rental throughout the United States. All outlets franchisee-owned, no corporate operations. The franchising is completely owned by franchisees, all officers and directors are franchisees.

Number of franchisees: 124 franchisees operating 267 locations in 41 states and the District of Columbia

In business since: 1968

Equity capital needed: Minimum $15,000, additional needed depends on potential of licensed area

Financial assistance available: Advertising support, national advertising program, national credit card programs, assistance in obtaining financing from lending institutions.

Training provided: Initial on-site training and continuing training through regularly scheduled meetings, seminars, and periodic business analysis.

Managerial assistance available: Managerial and technical assistance provided through comprehensive manuals and continuing updating and modification. Traveling representatives provide periodic business analysis, and the franchisor has available a computerized accounting system. Centralized international travel agency commission payment program and central billing is furnished.

BUDGET RENT A CAR CORPORATION
35 East Wacker Drive
Chicago, Illinois 60601
Attention: Franchise Department

Description of operation: Franchise of car and truck rental.

Number of franchisees: 1,700 locations: in all states, Canada, and world-wide

In business since: 1960

Equity capital needed: Varies with size of operation

Financial assistance available: Occasionally, depending on circumstances

Training provided: Management and operational training at the Budget training center, at selected locations and on-the-job.

Managerial assistance available: During the term of the franchise, Budget has full management team available to include legal, financial, franchise, operations, promotion, advertising, and insurance staffs.

COMPACTS ONLY RENT A CAR SYSTEM INC.
4785 Kipling
Wheatridge, Colorado 80033
James J. Scherer

Description of operation: Compacts Only Rent A Car System Inc. offers an opportunity in the daily automobile rental business. By taking a position in only the compact and subcompacts rental field a loyal following can be developed by people looking only for "reliable transportation at economical prices."

Number of franchisees: 12 in Nevada, California, Wyoming, Texas, Utah, and Arizona

In business since: 1969

Equity capital needed: $35,000

Financial assistance available: Financing can be arranged on automobiles through local or automobile credit companies

Training provided: Extension 3 weeks of training plus ongoing help as needed.

Managerial assistance available: Aid in surveying the market, setting rates. Continuing advertising in regional media. Toll-free reservation system. Toll-free access for continuing management advice.

DOLLAR RENT A CAR SYSTEMS, INC.
6141 West Century Boulevard
Los Angeles, California 90045
E. Woody Francis

Description of operation: Automobile and truck rental. Heavy concentration in airport operations.

Number of franchisees: Over 400 in the U.S. and Canada; over 1,250 Inter-Rent locations in Europe, Mexico, Mideast, and Africa

In business since: 1966

Equity capital needed: Approximately $100,000

Financial assistance available: Occasionally assists in financing.

Training provided: Standardized accounting system set up. Operational training by franchisor's representative at site.

Managerial assistance available: Assistance in-site selection. Standardized free-standing building. Consultant on-site during construction. Guidance in selection and balance of fleet. Continuing guidance in accounting and operations. Nationwide advertising campaign, co-op program available, and nationwide reservations service.

HERTZ SYSTEM, INC.
660 Madison Avenue
New York, New York 10021

Description of operation: Hertz System, Inc., offers franchises for the conduct of car and truck rental and leasing businesses in the United States under the "Hertz" name.

Number of franchisees: Over 1,100 car and truck rental locations in all states except Florida and Hawaii

In business since: 1918

Equity capital needed: Varies according to franchise-operating capital as required by location

Financial assistance available: None

Training provided: Zone System Manager trains new franchisee before operation opens with Hertz Starter Kit (kit includes all forms needed to run a location). Visits by system manager on a periodic basis. Manager rental representative training classes. Manuals and guides for running a location issued. Corporate training class available to franchisees. Annual business meeting.

Managerial assistance available: Accounting and operational guides are provided to run the location. Visits by corporate zone system manager to act as a liaison between the corporate and licensee locations. All forms and training classes provided as needed. Training and business meetings. Contact provided directly to corporate management for all areas of rental business (insurance, advertising, accounting, etc.).

HOLIDAY RENT-A-CAR SYSTEM
1400—66th Street, North
Suite 425
St. Petersburg, Florida 33710
George V. Durnin, General Manager

Description of operation: Automobile renting and leasing.

Number of franchisees: 72 in 24 States

In business since: 1975

Equity capital needed: $30,000

Financial assistance available: Assistance in establishing necessary lines of credit with which to acquire vehicles. Assistance in procuring fleet insurance.

Training provided: Theory complete with procedure manual, 1 day. On-the-job training, 5 days. Opening assistance and review, 5 days. Follow-up visit and review, 2–3 days.

Managerial assistance available: As much time as necessary in vehicle procurement, insurance procurement, office and counter procedures, customer qualification, hiring and training personnel, business development, advertising, accounting, vehicle disposal, and fleet maintenance procedures.

NATIONAL CAR RENTAL SYSTEM, INC.
5501 Green Valley Drive
Minneapolis, Minnesota 55437
Tom Bonner, Director of Operations Licensee Division

Description of operation: Automobile renting and leasing

Number of franchisees: 349 owning a total 948 franchises in all 50 states

In business since: 1947

Equity capital needed: Varies according to franchise operating capital required by location

Financial assistance available: Will accept promissory note for franchise fee.

Training provided: Initial training by field representative utilizing complete start-up kit. Comprehensive accounting program tailored to the car rental business.

Managerial assistance available: Periodic visits and phone contact by field representatives. Maintain regional offices to service and assist licensees in areas of fleet and revenue planning, marketing, accounting, and all phases of the business.

PAYLESS CAR RENTAL SYSTEM, INC.
1505 West 4th Street
Spokane, Washington 99204
L. E. Netterstrom, President

Description of operation: Payless Car Rental System, Inc., franchises companies or individuals to rent vehicles to the general public under the U.S. Registered Servicemark "Payless Car Rental System." Payless specializes in the rental of small economy cars at low rates with free mileage.

Number of franchisees: 107 franchise operations in 33 states, Canada, and Martinique

In business since: 1971

Equity capital needed: Franchisee will require a credit line to finance rental fleet plus $5,000 investment for a franchise in a city with a population of 200,000. Financing of receivables, deposits, various start-up costs varies.

Financial assistance available: The $5,000 investment pays for the franchise fee, training, all supplies and forms during first year of operation, signs (interior and exterior), and accounting system. Payless will assist the franchisee in obtaining a credit line from local banks, GMAC, Ford Motor Credit, etc.

Training provided: Payless agrees to furnish guidance to the franchisee in establishing, operating, and promoting the business of renting automobiles, with respect to: the institution and maintenance of office management systems and business operating procedures; the institution of a continuing sales campaign and securing a vehicle rental location and office.

Managerial assistance available: Payless provides a continuing relationship with its franchisees in the following ways: Franchisees are allowed to call the Payless National Headquarters collect as regards technical problems, reservation handling, insurance questions, and supply or advertising needs; Payless will make calls to franchisees' office to help franchisee improve and promote his rent-a-car business. A monthly newsletter and Operation Manual changes are mailed on a regular basis to franchise.

THRIFTY RENT-A-CAR SYSTEM
P.O. Box 35250
2400 North Sheridan Road
Tulsa, Oklahoma 74151
Cecil R. Davis, Franchise Director

Description of operation: Daily car rental business. Thrifty rents new, full size, midsize, compact, and subcompact automobiles to the general public at Thrifty rates.

Number of franchisees: Better than 400 locations in all 50 states, Puerto Rico, Canada, Scotland, England, Central America, Mexico, and Israel.

In business since: 1958

Equity capital needed: $25,000–$50,000

Financial assistance available: Franchisor assists licensee in setting up lines of credit for purchase of vehicles.

Training provided: On-the-job training 1 week in company-owned operation, 1 week with licensee at opening, and periodically thereafter.

Managerial assistance available: Franchisor furnishes continuing management and technical assistance to franchisee. Management assistance is under supervision of experienced, knowledgable supervisors who are full time employees of Thrifty Rent-A-Car System, Inc.

Beauty Salons/Supplies

EDIE ADAMS CUT & CURL
125 South Service Road
Long Island Expressway
Jericho, New York 11753
Don von Liebermann, Vice President

Description of operation: Operating of beauty salons with 12 to 20 stations under the Edie Adams Cut & Curl/Haircrafters.

Number of franchisees: 350 in 40 States

In business since: 1955

Equity capital needed: $40,000

Financial assistance available: Up to $25,000 financing to qualified applicants.

Training provided: In salon training about 10 days. Preopening training in franchisee's salon and complete supply of manuals.

Managerial assistance available: Home office, technical, seminars, new techniques, and management techniques.

THE BARBERS, HAIRSTYLING FOR MEN AND WOMEN, INC.
300 Industrial Boulevard
Minneapolis, Minnesota 55413

Description of operation: A completely systemized men's and women's hairstyling shop with inventory controls, accounting systems, advertising, public relations, business management programs, and turn-key built locations.

Number of franchisees: 80 in 17 states plus 35 company owned.

In business since: 1963

Equity capital needed: $20,000 to $35,000

Financial assistance available: Available to qualified applicants. Investor partners welcomed.

Training provided: Management and technical, 1 week, then quarterly seminars.

Managerial assistance available: Business management, including advertising, public relations, accounting and record keeping, training in hairstyling, and all related services.

COMMAND PERFORMANCE
First International Services Corporation
Westbank Boardwalk
Westport, Connecticut 06880
Steve Schimpff, Director of Marketing

Description of operation: Precision haircutting and styling salons for men and women. By employing a manager, most franchisees devote only 10–14 hours per week to the business.

Number of franchisees: 278 franchisees own 840 franchises in 42 states

In business since: 1976

Equity capital needed: Total cost to purchase, construct and open salon: $75,000 to $100,000.

Financial assistance available: Up to $25,000 of financing is available to qualified individuals.

Training provided: In addition to recruiting and training the shop's manager and staff, the franchisor conducts a comprehensive week-long training course for its franchisees in all phases of operations, advertising, promotion, legal and financial considerations.

Managerial assistance available: In addition to initial site selection, lease negotiations, hiring and training of staff, construction counsel, the franchisor furnishes continuing management, marketing, operational and technical assistance to franchisee and his employees.

GREAT EXPECTATIONS PRECISION HAIRCUTTERS
125 South Service Road
Long Island Expressway
Jericho, New York 11753
Don von Liebermann, Vice President

Description of operation: Great Expectations is a distinctive haircutting establishment primarily servicing men and women aged 18–34, appealing to the contemporary hair care customer. The franchise package offers: a thoroughly modern, attractively designed shop, streamlined equipment, operational support, training and personal recruitment.a4

Number of franchisees: 117 in 33 States

In business since: 1955

Equity capital needed: Total initial investment $72,500–$145,000

Financial assistance available: Financial assistance available up to $35,000 to qualified applicants.

Training provided: In salon training about 10 days. Preopening training in franchisee's salon and complete supply of manuals.

Managerial assistance available: Home office, technical seminars, new techniques, and management training. Advertising materials and promotions.

HAIR PERFORMERS
c/o John F. Amico & Co., Inc.
7327 West 90th Street
Bridgeview, Illinois 60455
Ronald Austin, Director of Sales

Description of operation: Family hair care center which provides styling and hair cutting for the entire family. Most franchisees operate store on limited hours (8 to 10). All business and management aids provided. Regional offices and training facilities throughout the U.S. Two basic schools in Chicago.

Number of franchisees: 50 franchised units in 10 States, plus 20 company-owned

In business since: 1962

Equity capital needed: $25,000 to $50,000

Financial assistance available: Up to $25,000 to qualified applicants.

Training provided: Staffing, recruiting, management selection and training provided for franchisee. Training conducted at home office, regional offices, company-owned college and in-store programs.

Managerial assistance available: Complete site selection, lease negotiations, salon design, full staffing and continual management assistance and full training at Hair Performers college.

KENNETH OF LONDON, LTD.
International Headquarters
1130 Burnett Avenue, Suite D
Concord, California 94520

Description of operation: Complete hairstyling studios for men, women, and children. Franchisor offers site selection and construction criteria. Interior design is standardized for all studios. Hairstylist and management recruiting and training is provided. Continuing education is provided through an audio/video program. Advertising is supported through a planned advertising program.

Number of franchisees: 11 in California

In business since: 1976

Equity capital needed: $60,000 to $95,000

Financial assistance available: None

Training provided: 1-week orientation and operations manual studies at corporate headquarters for franchisee.

Managerial assistance available: 2 to 3 weeks manager and stylist recruiting and system training at franchisee's location. Continuing provision of audio/video tapes in studio operation and hairstyling techniques in each studio.

MAGIC MIRROR INC.
11337 Ventura Boulevard
Studio City, California 91604
Dale Scott, President

Description of operation: Beauty salon cosmetics sold at retail (private brand).

Number of franchisees: 9 in California, New Jersey and Florida

In business since: 1949

Equity capital needed: $40,000–$60,000

Financial assistance available: Helps find financing.

Training provided: 2 weeks at headquarters, 1 week at franchisee's shop covering management and operation.

Managerial assistance available: Continuous training, counselor visits every 3 months providing assistance in accounting, operations, advertising and brand name merchandise. Franchisee may buy from other suppliers.

ROFFLER INDUSTRIES, INC.
400 Chess Street
Coraopolis, Pennsylvania 15108
Dr. Larry Casterline, Executive Director, Franchise Operations

Description of operation: Roffler Industries, Inc., formulates, manufactures and sells Roffler men's cosmetics and hair styling and hair care preparations for use throughout the U.S. by barbers trained in the Roffler Sculptur-Kut System of cutting and styling men's hair. Sales are made to 47 area distributors who in turn sell to approximately 8,000 barbers franchised as of January 31, 1978 by the company to use Roffler's name, hairstyling system and products and to sell Roffler products to the public. Roffler also manufactures and sells "Nu-Vita" and "Capilo" hair styling, hair care, and cosmetic products, and in addition sells barber equipment and supplies purchased from others, to its area distributors as well as to barber and beauty supply dealers generally.

Number of franchisees: Over 8,000 in all states

In business since: 1968

Equity capital needed: $495 to cover franchise fee, equipment, and inventory

Financial assistance available: None

Training provided: Hairstyling fashions can change from month to month, and Roffler takes great pride in not only keeping up-to-date in hairstyling trends but anticipating them months in advance. Local and national seminars, part of a franchise, provide the personalized education that each Roffler Pro needs to assure continuing success. Refresher clinics are an integral part of the seminars. Seminars include education in additional services as hairpiece fitting, cleaning, and coloring; hair and scalp treatments; facials, hair coloring, and hair straightening. These techniques are mastered by the Roffler Pros since they provided significant increases in income.

Managerial assistance available: The franchisor has no obligation during the operation of the business to give assistance to the franchisee in the operation of his business since, in almost every case, the franchisee is operating a barber shop already in operation. Franchisor and its area dealers do from time to time conduct training seminars.

S.M.R. ENTERPRISES, INC.
5703 Quince
Memphis, Tennessee 38117
Sam M. Ross, President

Description of operation: The company sells licenses for Fantastic Sam's Family Haircutters, a unique retail hair care establishment oriented to the demands, pocketbooks, and convenience of the typical American family.

Number of franchisees: 61 licensees are located in 22 states and operate 125 locations.

In business since: 1974

Equity capital needed: Approximately $48,000

Financial assistance available: A total investment of $48,000 is necessary to open a Fantastic Sam's license. The $15,000 license fee pays for market research, media planning, site location, lease negotiation, and extensive training; $18,000 is the recommended allocation for advertising and working capital; the remaining $15,000 is for furniture and fixtures, for which leasing arrangements are available.

Training provided: An intensive headquarters training course is supplemented by an additional week or more of preopening, start-up, and reinforcement training.

Managerial assistance available: Regional and in-shop seminars are provided on at least a quarterly basis. Regularly scheduled advance training programs for owners, managers, and cutters are offered at corporate headquarters. Consulting services are provided upon request by licensee or on an as-needed basis.

Business Aids/Services

AMERICAN ADVERTISING DISTRIBUTORS, INC.
1424 East Broadway
Mesa, Arizona 85204
Richard Elliott, President

Description of operation: American Advertising Distributors, Inc., has established techniques, methods, experience, and know-how in establishing a cooperative direct mail business. Franchisee shall have the exclusive marketing license for a territory. The company has facilities for the printing and production of coupons and other mailing pieces.

Number of franchisees: 50 in 19 states

In business since: 1976

Equity capital needed: $25,000 to $50,000 depending on population of territory

Financial assistance available: None

Training provided: 1 week of formal training school at the company's home office, 2 weeks of training at either a similar operation, or in the licensee's territory by a company representative.

Managerial assistance available: Provided for in training school.

AMERICAN DYNAMICS CORP.
Box 11, Cathedral Station
New York, New York 10025
Frank Forrester, General Manager

Description of operation: Financial Counselors educate clients and promote seminars to demonstrate benefits of (a) compounding savings @ 12 percent tax-free in 12 percent Savings Club; (b) deducting $1,750 off taxable income via IRS-approved IRA Master Pension Plan; (c) saving state sales tax on cars, machinery, and farm equipment; (d) avoiding probate court and estate and inheritance taxes with "Double Trusts;" (e) avoiding capital gains tax on investments via a U.S.-based, leased tax haven; (f) converting income to tax-free capital gains on all invoiced products, professional services, and future payments receivable including paychecks; and (g) providing 9 to 1 tax shelters.

Number of franchisees: 103 in 37 states

In business since: 1959

Equity capital needed: $150 for counselors; $500 for dealers

Financial assistance available: Franchisor has eliminated all normal licensing costs for the investment, tax shelter, and tax haven business.

Training provided: 70-page training manual plus cassette tapes. Further help by mail is free.

Managerial assistance available: The training manual solves all normal problems and answers typical questions. Also, it describes all services offered. New services and future improvements are covered in periodic newsletters, by correspondence, and by local seminars.

AMERICAN FACILITIES INSPECTION, INC.
300 Burntwood
North Little Rock Arkansas 72116
Royce A. Flynn, Secretary

Description of operation: An inspection service provided for prepurchase and facility condition evaluation pertaining to home, business, and industry. An Associate License is granted for a secured area for a nominal fee, for a period of 5 years, and renewable for $100. A percentage of amount charged for each inspection is paid as a royalty fee. Tool box, tools, business cards, invoices, price guides, and some advertisements are furnished.

Number of franchisees: 22 in 13 states

In business since: 1977

Equity capital needed: $2,000 to $5,000, plus $3,000 working capital

Financial assistance available: None

Training provided: A 3-day intensified training course provided to qualified personnel, with lodging paid at national headquarters, North Little Rock, Arkansas. Associates are carefully screened for character, and technical background with experience required in building maintenance, general knowledge of construction, quality control.

Managerial assistance available: Technical and manpower assistance available, standard bookkeeping system used. Periodic bulletins provided to improve both technical managerial operations.

ASSOCIATED TAX CONSULTANTS OF AMERICA, INC.
18552 MacArthur Boulevard, Suite 400
Irvine, California 92715
Paul A. Sax, Franchise Manager

Descripion of operation: Preparation of computerized income tax returns, bookkeeping, and financial planning. Company provides a complete marketing program for all three functions in addition to continuous training.

Number of franchisees: 52 in California, Nevada, Colorado, Utah, Minnesota, and Ohio

In business since: 1966

Equity capital needed: $17,000

Financial assistance available: Company will finance two-thirds upon approved credit.

Training provided: ATC will thoroughly train its franchisees in both federal and state personal income tax returns, along with basic bookkeeping knowledge and financial planning. ATC will aid in helping individuals obtain their NASD and Life & Disability Insurance Licenses. Typically, the new franchisees will receive in excess of 3 weeks training during their first year.

Managerial assistance available: Associated Tax Consultants provides continual management services for the life of the franchisee including but not limited to bookkeeping, advertising, training, procuring new clients, forms and procedures, location, training new consultants, computer updating, and sales.

AUDIT CONTROLS, INC.
87 Northeast 44th Street
Fort Lauderdale, Florida 33334
Arieh Douer, President

Description of operation: Nationwide collection service. No collection fees. Nominal service change. Trademark registered by the U.S. Patent Office #880, 919. Audit Controls, Inc., representatives are supplied with mailers (a direct advertising brochure) and a complete set-up for direct mail, magazine advertising, telephone soliciting, and direct sales.

Number of franchisees: 490 in 50 States

In business since: 1980

Equity capital needed: $100 for supplies

Financial assistance available: No financial assistance provided.

Training provided: No training required. Detailed instructions mailed to each representative.

Managerial assistance available: Free advisory assistance is available to representatives.

BEST RESUME SERVICE
The Penthouse
625 Stanwix Street
Pittsburgh, Pennsylvania 15222
Richard D. Hindman, President

Description of operation: Best Resume Service provides a broad range of professional business communication services for the educational, commercial, and individual client markets. These services include professional resume writing and printing, marketing proposals and brochures, direct mail processing, automatic typing, and word processing.

Number of franchisees: 26 in 16 states and Washington, D.C.

In business since: 1962

Equity capital needed: $5,000 to $25,000 depending on territory

Financial assistance available: Franchisor will finance, or arrange financing of, up to 50 percent of required capital for qualified franchisee's with good credit rating.

Training provided: Franchisor conducts a formal, intensive 2-week training program for all new franchisees in the corporate offices. Franchisee's managers may attend any scheduled training program at no charge. Update training seminars conducted periodically.

Managerial assistance available: Best Resume Service provides a continuous program of assistance to all franchisees in all phases of their business operations and management, finances and record keeping, marketing and personnel. Visits to the franchisee's office are made regularly by home office staff, and all franchisee's participate in periodic refresher training seminars. Market research and testing of new products and services is done continuously by the franchisor's home office.

BINEX-AUTOMATED BUSINESS SYSTEMS, INC.
1787 Tribute Road, Suite M
Sacramento, California 95815
Walter G. Heidig, President

Description of operation: Binex franchises offer a broad range of computerized services to small and medium-sized businesses. Services include financial reports, general ledgers, accounts receivable, accounts payable, job cost, payroll; specialized computer services are also available, and you can develop your own. You may operate your business in various ways from a bookkeeping office to a full computer service.

Number of franchisees: 60 in 21 states and Canada.

In business since: 1966

Equity capital needed: $7,500. The fee covers training, manuals, and start-up supplies. No expensive equipment is required.

Financial assistance available: None

Training provided: Home study course, 2-week home office and 1-week on-the-job. Franchisees may return for further training as needed. Complete operations manuals, technical manuals, and promotion manuals are provided.

Managerial assistance available: Support is provided on a continuous basis. Frequent newsletters are sent out covering a variety of subjects including business operation, marketing, technical, taxes, etc. New programs and services are developed, documented, and made available regularly to all franchisees. Periodic regional meetings provide upgrading and review.

H & R BLOCK, INC.
4410 Main Street
Kansas City, Missouri 64111
William T. Ross, Vice President; Director, Administrative Operations

Description of operation: The exclusive function of H & R Block, Inc., is to prepare individual income tax returns. The franchise is operated in a city by an individual or partnership. The only warranty made by the franchisee is to respect and uphold a specific code of ethics and to abide by the policy and procedures of the company.

Number of franchisees: Over 8,000 offices throughout the United States, Canada, and 13 foreign countries. Over 4,000 offices are franchised with the balance operated by the parent company.

In business since: 1946

Equity capital needed: $1,000 to $2,000

Financial assistance available: None

Training provided: Each year a training program is held in November for all new managers. Prior to tax season each year, a training program for all employees is conducted in major centers. Each summer a meeting is held for all managers for 3 days to discuss all phases of the operation and new developments and ideas.

Managerial assistance available: We work very closely with our franchisees and provide any and all assistance required or needed.

BUSINESS BROKERAGE INVESTMENT GROUP
42 Weybosset Street
Providence, Rhode Island 02903

Description of operation: Business Brokerage Group offices are licensees of the Business Brokerage Investment Group, Inc. Each office has an owner/manager which specializes exclusively in business sales, mergers, and acquisitions of proprietorships, partnerships, and corporations with gross annual sales of $2 million dollars or less. The total number of small businesses sold each year creates a strong market and is the basis of BBG's activity.

Number of franchisees: 25 in 7 states with offices scheduled to be opened throughout the country.

In business since: 1977

Equity capital needed: $20,000 plus $5,000 operating capital

Financial assistance available: Yes, to qualified individuals.

Training provided: On-the-job training which includes all phases of operation, 2-week courses at home office, plus training for duration necessary after opening as deemed required by individual.

Managerial assistance available: Training is on-going. Initial managerial and technical assistance provided for continuous period after office opening. Continuous telephone contact, site visits, and management assistance designed to support each licensee as needed. Periodic home-office conducted training seminars with required attendance by licensees.

BUSINESS CONSULTANTS OF AMERICA
Affiliate of: HORIZONS OF AMERICA
P.O. Box 4098
Waterbury, Connecticut 06714
Gregg Nolan, Franchise Director

Description of operation: Franchisor offers time-tested practice, dealing with advisory services for small and medium-sized business operations. Training in services to include; management, marketing, sales tax advisory, and financial advisory services. Additional training includes programs for mergers/acquisition, business brokerage, and estate planning.

Number of franchisees: 14 in 9 states and Canada

In business since: 1973

Equity capital needed: $8,500 plus $5,000 working capital

Financial assistance available: Assistance with bank/government financing.

Training provided: 2 weeks intensive training at franchise headquarters, followed by 2 months cassette courses packaged by franchisor and other professional organizations. Continuing franchisor advisory newsletters and tapes.

Managerial assistance available: First year, nonfee technical and advisory services at discretion of franchisee. Continued services on an as needed fee basis from franchisor. Additional memberships arranged in professional associations.

BUSINESS DATA SERVICES, INC.
1867 Crane Ridge Drive
Jackson, Mississippi 39216
W. D. Whigham, President

Description of operation: BDS licensees provide a complete computerized accounting and financial advisory service to a wide spectrum of small to medium-sized businesses. Services which the licensees provide include bookkeeping, tax preparation, and related financial planning and analysis.

Number of franchisees: 30 in 11 states

In business since: 1972, franchising since 1979

Equity capital needed: $14,500

Training provided: All required first-year training expenses, including transportation and accommodations, are borne by the licensor. Completion of a prerequisite home study course is required before the new licensee attends a 3-week central office initial training seminar. Additionally, BDS provides field training in licensee's area, together with in-field follow-up for the first year at licensor's expense. Licensee must attend a 4-day post graduate training course after the first year covering operations and marketing management.

Managerial assistance available: Complete and continuous support is provided to licensee. Central office maintains regular communications with licensee in the form of newsletters, seminars, and periodic personal visits at licensee's office. BDS staff is constantly available for telephone inquiry on technical and tax questions. A toll-free number is used by licensees to communicate with marketing director and staff CPA concerning client acquisition and technical areas.

SIMPLIFIED BUSINESS SERVICES, INC.
100 Presidential Boulevard
Bala Cynwyd, Pennsylvania 19004
Martin B. Miller, President

Description of operation: Simplified Business Services, Inc., offers bookkeeping systems and services that have been refined and developed over 44 years. These systems are designed for the small businessman who must keep records and who cannot afford a full-time CPA. The licensee can sell the system with or without monthly bookkeeping service and with or without tax preparation services.

Number of franchisees: 30 in 8 states and Washington, D.C.

In business since: 1934

Equity capital needed: No franchise fee

Financial assistance available: No inventory purchase limit is required.

Training provided: Sales training available from various licensees. Bookkeeping training available at home office.

Managerial assistance available: Business and tax advisory bulletins on regular basis. Licensee may call or write home office for advice at any time.

SMI INTERNATIONAL, INC.
(SUCCESS MOTIVATION INSTITUTE, INC.)
5000 Lakewood Drive
Waco, Texas 76710
Charles G. Williams

Description of operation: The company's international distributorship organization markets specialized management, sales, and personal development programs to individuals, companies, governments, and other organizations. Materials are printed and recorded, using modern learning methods, personal goal setting, and management-by-objective techniques.

Number of franchisees: 1,898 in 50 states and 23 foreign countries

In business since: 1960

Equity capital needed: $12,950

Financial assistance available: Financial assistance provided.

Training provided: Complete distributorship training program in printed and recorded form furnished with initial investment; continuous home office sales training and sales management seminars available monthly. Field sales training also available in many areas without cost to distributors.

Managerial assistance available: Continuous sales consultant assistance provided by home office to distributors through use of monthly mailings, company-owned WATS lines, and prompt response to mail communications.

WHITEHILL SYSTEMS
Division of SMALL BUSINESS ADVISORS, INC.
12 Franklin Place
Woodmere, New York 11598
Larry Speizman, President

Description of operation: A nationwide organization devoted to counseling small and medium-sized businesses with emphasis on recordkeeping systems, computerized programs, and tax service. The programs include complete, easy to maintain, preprinted manual, one-write or computerized recordkeeping system, custom designed to provide a monthly profit and loss statement and proof of accuracy, meeting requirements of the Internal Revenue Service. Locally authorized business counselors review and analyze recordkeeping requirements; furnish a complete set of records; provide personal instructions on use and maintenance of records;

analyze records and financial statements; provide guidance throughout the year. Federal and state income tax returns are prepared with a guarantee of accuracy by professional staff at the national office. Tax specialists in national office provide tax advisory service and answer income tax questions, publish a monthly tax and business bulletin including up-to-date tax information and money-saving ideas.

Number of franchisees: Franchises in 48 states

In business since: 1974

Equity capital needed: $15,000, includes training, cost of starting inventory, supply of sales and promotional literature, initial direct mail campaign. A $10,000 life insurance policy premium (paid for the first year).

Financial assistance available: Limited

Training provided: 6 days training at home office at company expense, in all phases of the system and selling methods. Five days field training in distributor's own territory, with experienced representative, at company expense.

Managerial assistance available: Retraining program and continuous assistance as needed.

EDWIN K. WILLIAMS & CO.
5324 Ekwill Street
P.O. Box 6406
Santa Barbara, California 93111
Gene H. Loeppke, Vice President, Field Operations

Description of operation: Edwin K. Williams & Company provides business management counseling and computerized bookkeeping services to small business through a franchised licensee program that combines two systems in one franchise: (1) Edwin K. Williams & Company offers these services exclusively for service station retailers and petroleum wholesalers (jobbers); Edwin K. Williams & Company specialized recordkeeping systems are recommended by over 30 oil companies; and (2) E-Z Keep Systems, a division of Edwin K. Williams & Company serves all other types of small business.

Number of franchisees: 260 licensee offices in the United States

In business since: 1935

Equity capital needed: $8,000 to $25,000 & up (depending upon size of territory being purchased)

Financial assistance available: Limited

Training provided: New licensees are provided initial training, including training in existing licensee offices, plus training and guidance by the company's regional managers after installation. A continuing program of training seminars is offered to all licensees. Subjects include internal procedures, taxes, business management counseling, E.D.P. and more.

Managerial assistance available: Regional managers provide continued follow-up counseling in all phases of licensee operation. The home office field operations staff provides technical support and other assistance.

Cosmetics/Toiletries

CHRISTINE VALMY, INC.
767 Fifth Avenue
New York, New York 10022
Henry D. Sterian, Chairman of Board
Judith O'Connell, Franchise Sales Director

Description of operation: Christine Valmy, Inc., offers a totally vertical skin care salon franchise package and manufactures its own skin care machines, apparatus, bulk and retail products for a retail salon operation. Each salon is approximately 1,200 square feet and is open about 8 hours daily, 6 days a week. An extensive inventory of Christine Valmy products and skin care equipment is maintained in each salon.

Number of franchisees: 20 in 9 states

In business since: 1964

Equity capital needed: Approximately $75,000

Financial assistance available: A 50 percent deposit of franchise fee ($10,000) is required upon commitment, and balance of fee due upon signing license agreement. Balance due on total investment upon salon opening.

Training provided: Intensive 4–5 week mandatory skin care and makeup course for salon owner/manager and two skin care specialists (estheticians) given at the Christine Valmy International School for Esthetics, Skin Care & Makeup (licensed by the New York State Board of Education).

Managerial assistance available: Managerial assistance provided in-site selection, salon design/layout, public relations, grand opening promotions, textbook and operational manuals, monthly newsletters. Manager/owner can observe daily activities of flagship Fifth Avenue Salon and work closely with salon director. Technical and managerial training plus yearly refresher and update training course.

COLOR ME BEAUTIFUL COSMETICS
P.O. Box 52
North Hackensack Station
River Edge, New Jersey 07661
Irving Davidoff

Description of operation: The investment includes 20 sales locations, 20 merchandise showcase units and an opening inventory (retail value—$12,800). Licensees are selected to service retail outlets who display and sell Color Me Beautiful cosmetics.

Number of franchisees: 10 in Connecticut, New York, and New Jersey

In business since: 1960

Equity capital needed: $11,900

Financial assistance available: None

Training provided: Complete indoctrination in the product and merchandising promotions on an ongoing basis. Continuous field supervision to insure optimum sales and profits to the licensee.

Managerial assistance available: Company assists in set up of showcase units and merchandise and provides advertising and publicity promotions.

FASHION TWO TWENTY, INC.
1263 South Chilicothe Road
Aurora, Ohio 44202
Ray A. Curtiss, Vice President, Sales

Description of operation: Fashion Two Twenty, Inc., has a prestige line of cosmetics that are introduced to the customer through the party plan. They offer a wholesale training and distribution center operation to those people who have a direct sales background and have the ability to motivate people and form a sales force.

Number of franchisees: Approximately 800 throughout the entire United States

In business since: 1962

Equity capital needed: $1,300 for initial inventory package

Financial assistance available: Cash basis

Training provided: 3 days of concentrated schooling plus workshops and sales seminars twice a year

Managerial assistance available: In addition to expert guidance, the home office provides recordkeeping support, effective sales aids, brochures, recruiting and training films, and weekly and monthly publications recognizing organizations, national advertising, contests, promotions, car program for qualified managers, and sales meetings.

I NATURAL COSMETICS
NUTRIENT COSMETIC LTD.
820 Shames Drive
Westbury, New York 11590
Robert B. Greenberg, Executive Vice President

Description of operation: Unique retail operation of a cosmetic boutique specializing in customer service and education primarily located in regional, fashion malls, shopping centers, and downtown areas. Products based on natural ingredients and merchandizing includes out-of-shop demonstrations, classes, and shows. Only products offered are i Natural cosmetics.

Number of franchisees: 60 in 21 states

In business since: 1970

Equity capital needed: Total capital required $40,000 to $50,000 depending on location

Financial assistance available: No financial assistance provided.

Training provided: Formal classroom program held at site of retail location for staff, manager and owner. Minimum of 1 week.

Managerial assistance available: Training includes operations, selling techniques, promotional programs, and shop administrators. Our training staff visits each franchised shop generally once each calendar quarter for training in new products, refresher courses, and problem solving.

JUDITH SANS INTERNATIONALE, INC.
3867 Roswell Road Northeast
Atlanta, Georgia 30342
Judith Sans, President

Description of operation: Skin care and cosmetic centers.

Number of franchisees: 8 in 6 states

Equity capital needed: $70,000

Financial assistance available: None

Training provided: 14 days intensive training provided by franchisor at training headquarters in Atlanta, Georgia.

Managerial assistance available: Continuous

LADY BURD EXCLUSIVE COSMETICS, INC.
158–01 Crossbay Boulevard
Howard Beach, New York 11414

Description of operation: Wholesale and retail cosmetics featuring services as facials, manicures, pedicures, body waxing, (electrolyses and depilation hair removal) also haircutting. (Private Label Cosmetics.)

Number of franchisees: 3 in New York

In business since: 1960

Equity capital needed: $5,000–$10,000 depending on location. Many start in home and when established, move to a store.

Financial assistance available: None

Training provided: We train completely. Can take 1 to 3 days of basic training.

Managerial assistance available: All help needed in guidance on how to run your operation.

SYD SIMONS COSMETICS, INC.
2 East Oak Street
Chicago, Illinois 60611
Jerome Weitzel, President

Description of operation: Syd Simons Cosmetics offers a unique completely equipped makeup and skin care studio for the sale of a complete line of cosmetic products and accessories as well as related services. The package includes all furniture, fixtures, studio supplies, opening inventory, decorating, brochures, and advertising and promotional materials.

Number of franchisees: 6 in Illinois, Kansas, and California

In business since: Retailing 1940, franchising 1972

Equity capital needed: Approximately $30,000

Financial assistance available: Franchisor will assist franchise in obtaining business loan from appropriate lending institution.

Training provided: Syd Simons Cosmetics provides basic 60-day training period in makeup and skin care as well as studio operations and business procedures at the franchisor's home office. Additional on-site training conducted periodically.

Managerial assistance available: Syd Simons provides continual managerial, legal, financial, and promotional guidance in accordance with the needs of the franchisee, as well as assistance in sales areas.

Drug Stores

LE$-ON RETAIL SYSTEMS, INC.
dba LE$-ON DRUGS
5301 West Dempster Street
Skokie, Illinois 60077
Leslie B. Masover, President

Description of operation: Retail drug stores.

Number of franchisees: 28 in Illinois

In business since: 1968

Equity capital needed: $10,000 to $50,000 depending on size of store and type

Financial assistance available: Counsel and introduction to banking sources.

Training provided: Minimum 2 weeks of training.

Managerial assistance available: Managerial assistance provided for duration of license agreement.

MEDICINE SHOPPES INTERNATIONAL, INC.
10121 Paget Drive
St. Louis, Missouri 63162
Edwin F. Prizer, President

Description of operation: Retail sales of pharmaceuticals and medicines, emphasing ethics, professionalism, and profits.

Number of franchisees: 320 in 44 states

In business since: 1971

Equity capital needed: Investment $40,000, which includes fee, fixtures, opening inventory, and opening promotion

Financial assistance available: Lease package for fixtures, etc.

Training provided: 5-day training seminar at corporate headquarters. Two days or longer store opening assistance.

Managerial assistance available: Continuous in-training program for marketing and store operations. We furnish computerized bookkeeping and marketing services and financial and operational analysis on a monthly basis. Assistance in site selection, lease negotiation, store layout, fixturing, personnel selection, and purchasing procedures.

Educational Products/Services

ALLSTATE CONTRACTORS SCHOOLS TRAINING CENTERS
16661 Ventura Boulevard
Suite 120
Encino, California 91436
Don Van Kempen, President

Description of operation: Allstate Contractor Schools are in the private adult education field, whereby we assist individuals in passing the State Contractors License examination. Our method for instruction is by closed circuit television. Each student is provided a program to follow for his particular category of contracting.

Number of franchisees: 17 in California only

In business since: 1976

Equity capital needed: $8,500

Financial assistance available: First year license fee is $19,500. Paid $8,500 for set-up with equipment, films, and training. These monies are placed in impound until licensor performs. The balance is paid in 11 equal monthly payments of $1,000 per month. Licensee may terminate at anytime, 30 days written notice.

Training provided: 2 weeks home office stay for familiarization training in all facets of operation.

Managerial assistance available: Continuing guidance for the length of the license agreement, upgrading of curriculum as needed.

ALLSTATE REAL ESTATE LICENSE SCHOOL
16661 Ventura Boulevard
Suite 120
Encino, California 91436

Description of Operation: Allstate Real Estate License School is in the private adult education field where we assist individuals in passing the State Real Estate Sales exam. We use closed circuit television as a method of instruction.

Number of Franchisees: 9 in California only

In business since: 1977

Equity capital needed: $2,500

Financial Assistance Available: First year license fee is $4,900. Paid $2,500 for set-up with equipment, films, and training. These monies are placed in impound until licensor performs. The balance is paid in installments of $200 a month for 11 months. Licensee may terminate with 30 days written notice.

Training provided: 2 weeks home office stay for familiarization training in all facets of operation.

Managerial assistance available: Continuing guidance for the length of the license agreement, upgrading of curriculum as needed.

ANTHONY SCHOOLS
4401 Birch Street
P.O. Box 2960
Newport Beach, California 92663

Description of operation: The men and women who own and operate Anthony Schools franchises are involved in one of the most satisfying, personally rewarding fields of private education preparing adults for licenses and new career opportunities in real estate, contracting, insurance, and securities. Schools, which vary in size from 2,000 to 6,000 square feet and larger, are located in high quality shopping centers offering both day and evening classes. Franchisor writes, publishes, and prints the full educational product line of Anthony Schools courses, and updates them continuously for the franchisees students. Anthony Schools does not franchise outside of California.

Number of franchisees: 5 in California. These are master franchises operating 35 of the 50 California locations.

In business since: 1945

Equity capital needed: Varies widely with number of schools franchisee wishes to operate and size/location of marketing area. Complete financial statements and excellent credit rating required.

Financial assistance available: None

Training provided: In-depth training provided as long as required in all business and education phases, from initial marketing survey and site location studies to school operations, advertising, management, personnel selection and training, accounting, and instructional resources.

Managerial assistance available: Continuous management advice and assistance is provided for the duration of the franchise, covers functions of all school operations, all Anthony educational products, industry trends and data/information/guidance in education, administration, marketing, state and federal regulatory agencies. Franchise meetings, field consultations, and headquarters visits provide continuing management guidance and operating assistance.

AUDIO VISUAL EDUCATIONAL SYSTEMS
6116 Skyline Drive
P.O. Box 22768
Houston, Texas 77027
Leonard J. Blumenthal, Vice President/Franchise Development

Description of operation: Sales of audio visual equipment and supplies and video equipment and supplies to specific territory. All markets within such territory. Inventory, shipments, accounting, credit management to be maintained by national headquarters; monthly reports sent to franchisee.

Number of franchisees: 3 in 3 states

In business since: 1963

Equity capital needed: $25,000

Financial assistance available: Up to 40 percent of equity capital required.

Training provided: 1-week training at Houston franchise headquarters; 1-week training in franchise territory; daily communication by telephone to Houston headquarters.

Managerial assistance available: Once a quarter review in franchisee's territory for 1 or 2 days, more frequently if circumstances require.

BARBIZON SCHOOLS OF MODELING
3 East 54th Street
New York, New York, 10022
B. Wolff, Executive Vice President

Description of operation: Barbizon operates modeling and personal development schools for teen-age girls, homemakers, and career girls. The schools also offer a male modeling program, fashion merchandising course, acting course; and sell Barbizon cosmetics. We are the largest organization in this field.

Number of franchisees: 66 in 28 states

In business since: 1939

Equity capital needed: $25,000–$50,000

Financial assistance available: Franchisee can finance 50 percent of franchise fee with franchisor. Total franchise fee is $19,500 to $35,000.

Training provided: Intensive 3-week training program for franchisee and his director at corporate office. Extensive on-site field visits at franchisee's location by home office staff during first 6 months. Periodic staff visits and conferences at home office thereafter on a continuing basis.

Managerial assistance available: In addition to initial training indicated above, Barbizon makes available continuing staff programs, sales aids, new programs, brochures, direct mail pieces, etc.

UP-GRADE EDUCATIONAL SERVICES, INC.
2745 Carley Court
North Bellmore, New York 11710
Victoria Levy, President

Description of operation: Private and institutional tutoring and teaching. Provides teachers for all subjects and all levels. Specializing in individualized programs for children with "Learning Disabilities." Work is done in cooperation with hospitals, mental institutions, drug rehabilitation programs, pediatricians, psychologists, and psychiatrists, in institutions or privacy of individual's own home. All teachers that are recommended are certified or licensed in specialized areas. Can be fully operated from franchisee's home by professional and business-oriented individuals.

Number of franchisees: 17 in metropolitan New York area, franchises limited

In business since: 1964, Incorporated in 1969

Equity capital needed: $7,500 and up according to size of geographic area

Financial assistance available: 60 percent on closing, balance to be paid within 1 year.

Training provided: Training initially in home office, concentrated in less than 1 week. Operational manual. Training unlimited.

Managerial assistance available: Continuous assistance as necessary—no time limit. Each franchisee is required to attend at least one group meeting a year. Newsletters are sent out at least six times a year, suggesting new business ideas and programs experimented with that proved successful in an area. Franchisees are responsible for most of the material in Newsletter so there is a continuous exchange of ideas to develop and expand his business.

Employment Services

AAA EMPLOYMENT FRANCHISE, INC.
400—83rd Avenue North
St. Petersburg, Florida 33702
Thelma Ramey, Executive Vice President

Description of operation: AAA Employment Franchise, Inc., offers a highly ethical and professional service to both applicants and employers. AAA offices do not limit themselves to specialized areas of employment. Full service is available—executive to domestic placement—both temporary and permanent employment. The low placement fee of only 2 weeks salary has proven to be in great demand for the past 20 years. Coast to coast, border to border territories available on a first to qualify basis.

Number of franchisees: 7 in Arizona, Pennsylvania, Tennessee, and South Carolina

In business since: AAA Employment, Inc., 1957; AAA Employment Franchise, Inc., 1977

Equity capital needed: Down payment depends on size of territory selected (minimum $2,000, maximum $10,000) and approximately $3,000 (includes office space, furnishings, office supplies, and licensing)

Financial assistance available: Once down payment is made, the balance of the fee is paid $100 per month until paid off. No finance charge.

Training provided: The franchisor's staff provides the franchisee with an intensive 2-week training program at the corporate headquarters in St. Petersburg, Florida. Additional on-the-job training conducted in the field for the franchisee and employees. A representative from the home office spends the first week of operation in the franchisees office to offer assistance. Seminars are held semiannually to keep franchisees updated on new ideas and techniques.

Managerial assistance available: The staff of the franchisor provides the franchisee with continual support and assistance. Some of the services provided by the franchisor are: (1) aid in selecting a prime location, (2) aid in negotiating a lease, (3) providing information and research requirements for city, county, and state licenses, (4) selection of office furniture and supplies, (5) establishing an advertising schedule, (6) establishing a budget schedule, (7) hiring and training employees, and (8) record keeping. In addition to the continual communication between the franchisee and franchisor by phone, and the continued furnishing of information through the mail, visits are made periodically into the field by a representative of the corporation. The franchisee is also provided with a detailed operations manual as well as other reference guides. Every effort is made by AAA Employment Franchise, Inc.

ACME PERSONNEL SERVICE
P.O. Box 14466
Opportunity, Washington 99214
D. Scott MacDonald, Franchise Director

Description of operation: We have company-owned and franchised offices, operating to serve both applicant and employer clients in the placement of permanent personnel in all fields, from minimum wage up to upper level recruiting at income levels of $15,000–$50,000 or more. For permanent placements from minimum wage to $15,000 annual income, business is handled through "Acme Personnel Service." For employer-paid recruiting of permanent personnel in the salary range of $15,000 annual income on up, business is handled through "The Executive Suite." Territories are protected and need not be renewed.

Number of franchisees: 83 in 17 states

In business since: 1946

Equity capital needed: Franchise fee is from $9,500 to $19,500 depending on the size of the market territory. We recommend from 50–100 percent for support capital.

Financial assistance available: We may be able to recommend a prospective franchisee to suitable financing sources, if they should be needed. We also participate in national co-op advertising in franchisee's market on a 50-50 basis, up to a maximum.

Training provided: Before opening the office, franchisee receives a unique, concentrated, 1-week training course. Franchisee is given and taught how to use our 400-page company guide, which contains the essence of over 30 years of experience. Franchisee is also trained to use our system of personnel placement, as well as all internal procedures necessary to the successful running of the business. Within 90 days after opening, franchisee receives a personal visit from the franchise director and/or corporate district manager. Annual conventions are full of training sessions. Franchisee returns to 1-week training course every 3 years.

Managerial assistance available: Continual assistance from the franchise director and/or corporate district managers in franchisee's area in advertising, applicant recruitment, job-order promotion, internal staffing and training, bookkeeping, and other internal operations, etc. All new forms, procedures, ideas, and aids of any sort whatever are sent to franchisee on a regular basis, usually weekly. Franchisees receive free national advertising exposure, free job-order promotion materials sent into their markets quarterly, and other assistance as requested.

ADIA TEMPORARY SERVICES, INC.
64 Willow Place
Menlo Park, California 94025
Leonard N. Swartz, Vice President, Finance and Treasurer

Description of operation: Furnishing skilled office, technical, sales, and marketing personnel and industrial workers to clients on temporary, as needed, basis.

Number of franchisees: 39 in 17 states and South America

In business since: 1957

Equity capital needed: $25,000 plus, depending on market size

Financial assistance available: Franchisor finances entire temporary help payroll.

Training provided: 1 full week of formal, centralized, manager and staff training with additional field training provided immediately after office opening. Provides complete operating manuals on ADIA Temporary Help System.

Managerial assistance available: Continued headquarters guidance through weekly newsletter and bimonthly, monthly, and quarterly reports. Constant field training follow-up visits; national and regional seminars. Advice and assistance in such areas as advertising, marketing, insurance, financing, and sales.

BAILEY EMPLOYMENT SYSTEM, INC.
51 Shelton Road
Monroe, Connecticut 06468
Sheldon Leighton, President

Description of operation: Profitable, nationally scoped, placement techniques augmented with a centralized, electronically computerized, data retrieval system. Centrally filed applicants and centrally filed job specifications, registered by individual Bailey Employment System offices, allows all franchisees a constant pool of qualified applicants and employers with which to work at all times.

Number of franchisees: 20 in 5 states

In business since: 1960

Equity capital needed: $25,000

Financial assistance available: If desired, purchase price may be financed at going bank rates.

Training provided: Complete training in the profitable operation of a Bailey Employment Service office is given to each franchise operator before a new office is opened for business. Our training courses may be audited again and again by the franchise operator and his or her staff at their convenience. Additional training in advanced techniques of professional placement is offered 52 weeks a year. All such additional training is offered during nonworking hours and is free of charge to all franchise operators and personnel. Conventions are held at least 4 weekends a year to insure continued interoffice cooperations, comradery, and profits.

Managerial assistance available: Every conceivable service to insure the owner a profitable return on his or her investment is offered. Experts in site selection, advertising, and public relations, business procedures, and placement techniques, accounting and bookkeeping, teaching and instructional services, as well as on-site field representatives are maintained on the payroll of the parent company for the benefit of the franchise operators.

BAKER & BAKER EMPLOYMENT SERVICE, INC.
P.O. Box 364, 114–1/2 Washington Avenue
Athens, Tennessee 37303
Kathleen Baker, President

Description of operation: Franchising of employment service agencies for small towns of 20,000 population and city suburbs.

Number of franchisees: 20 offices open in 8 states

In business since: 1967

Equity capital needed: $8,000 to $10,000 dependent on location, plus $1,500 working capital

Financial assistance available:

Training provided: Comprehensive training course before opening and additional periodical on-the-job training at the franchise location.

Managerial assistance available: Selection of suitable locations, a nationally aimed public-relations program, and instructions and materials for obtaining maximum publicity in local advertising media, all forms required for the first 12 months of operation, an established accounting system, national placement Tele-System operating between offices, assistance in interpreting state laws and complying with license regulations. Trained assistance on call at all hours on any agency problem.

BRYANT BUREAU
A Division of SNELLING AND SNELLING, INC.
Executive Offices
4000 South Tamiami Trail
Sarasota, Florida 33581
William G. Allin, Group Vice President

Description of operation: Offers professional placement and recruiting services in technical, managerial, sales, and executive levels to qualified candidates.

Number of franchisees: 49 in 27 states

In business since: 1976 (parent company since 1951)

Equity capital needed: $25,000 to $100,000 plus

Financial assistance available: None

Training provided: 2 weeks training at home office in Sarasota, Florida, plus additional training in the field for franchisee and franchisee's employees. Franchisee's employees may be sent at any time free of charge to training classes given in Sarasota and throughout the country. Training includes the use of copyrighted training manuals for the director, staffing specialists, and the registrar; and a video systems training center that gives each licensee a powerful additional tool for reinforcing the skill of each staffing specialist.

Managerial assistance available: Assistance in all facets of preopening, site selection, survey, phone installation, office layout, and design plus continued communication through various media along with periodic field visits.

BUSINESS & PROFESSIONAL CONSULTANTS, INC.
3807 Wilshire Boulevard
Los Angeles, California 90010
W. J. LaPerch, President

Description of operation: Operates in the executive search, recruitment, and placement of managerial and executive talent at the professional level. Covers engineering, banking, insurance, accounting, finance, data processing, sales, marketing, and management personnel. All recruiting fees are derived from client company. Where state law permits, does not operate as an employment agency but as executive recruiters. The ideal franchise owner will come from industry at the middle to senior management level, will be degreed or equivalent (an advanced degree is desirable), will be people-oriented, will work well as part of a national team, and yet be capable of individual accomplishment and leadership. An additional facet of this franchise is the inclusion of a professional level temporary service to serve the same customer base and thus be able to satisfy all of the customer's needs. The company finances and handles all details of payroll and billing for the franchisee, so no large amount of payroll capital is required.

Number of franchisees: 8 in California

In business since: 1961

Equity capital needed: $10,000 franchise fee

Financial assistance available: Will finance portion of franchise fee at no interest.

Training provided: An initial 2-week program at the home office to cover the basics of executive search, hiring, and training of staff personnel, operational and accounting procedures, and market penetration. This is followed by an on-site training program of 1 full week at the franchisee's location, and by further field visits by home office training personnel.

Managerial assistance available: Continuous on an as-needed basis and may consist of seminars, field visits, refresher training at franchisor's home office, and constant communication.

HERITAGE PERSONNEL SYSTEMS, INC.
2920 Highwoods Boulevard
P.O. Box 95025
Raleigh, North Carolina 27625
Robert A. Hounsell, Direct of Franchising

Description of operation: Full service, "across the board" personnel employment agencies, serving all job-seekers from minimum wage to top executives in all job categories, on both a "company-paid fee" and "applicant-paid fee" basis, with marketing emphasis throughout the Southeast. Heritage's applicant interchange provides a continuous service to those franchisees desiring exposure of their specialized positions throughout the system.

Number of franchisees: 6 in North Carolina and Tennessee

In business since: 1974; began franchising in 1977

Equity capital needed: $7,500–$30,000 initial franchise fee, plus approximately $3,000 start-up costs

Financial assistance available: Possibility of company-financing of up to 50 percent of franchise fee, and advice and consultation in obtaining other sources of financial assistance.

Training provided: 2 weeks at company headquarters; 1 week in franchisee's office; continuous consultancy and assistance thereafter.

Managerial assistance available: Continuous assistance to franchisee in advertising, marketing, hiring, and training of staff, accounting, legal, office expansion, and new job market development. Close cooperation in the system's management-by-objectives procedures is maintained by phone, mail, and personal visits.

KOGEN PERSONNEL INC.
202 Whitemarsh Plaza
Conshohocken, Pennsylvania 19428
S. David Davis, President

Description of operation: Franchise provides full service through placement of one or more of the following levels: placement of permanent and temporary clerical and staff support applicants; placement of entry level sales, administrative and technical applicants; placement of middle-management, engineering and professional applicants; and searches for executive and key personnel for $40,000 to $200,000 positions.

Number of franchisees: 25 in 12 states

In business since: 1966

Equity capital needed: $20,000 minimum, depending upon location and personal objectives

Financial assistance available: Franchise charge may be financed in part

Training provided: Franchisee receives extensive preopening instruction in basic business management, followed by detailed and hands-on instruction and training in all levels of the business. Instruction and training is provided over a period of several months for maximum effectiveness. Training courses are continuously available throughout the year.

Managerial assistance available: Assistance in any area of agency operation and at every level is readily available. New ideas and procedures are discussed and distributed monthly through two house organs (one for management; one for consultants). Resumes and job orders are distributed throughout the system through its unique intrasystem alert.

Food-Grocery/Specialty Stores

AUGIE'S INC.
1900 West County Road C
St. Paul, Minnesota 55113
Ray Augustine, President

Description of operation: Industrial catering. Special equipped trucks to serve hot foods to workers on-the-job.

Number of franchisees: 60 in Minnesota

In business since: 1958

Equity capital needed: $1,000, some instances less

Financial assistance available: Weekly payment on amount due.

Training provided: Approximately 1-week training in driving and sales.

Managerial assistance available: Same as above.

THE BIG CHEESE, INC.
P.O. Box 33456
Phoenix, Arizona 85067
Arthur L. Thruston, Director of Marketing

Descripton of operation: We develop complete turn-key cheese and wine stores as a management consultant company, which allows a prospective buyer most advantages of a franchise without on-going costs of royalties, overrides, percentages, etc.

Number of franchisees: 23 in Arizona, California, Texas, and Montana

In business since: 1968

Equity capital needed: Approximately $30,000

Financial assistance available: It takes approximately $60,000 to $65,000 to open a Big Cheese operation. $30,000 or approximately one half cash required as a down payment and the balance financed through equipment lease purchase.

Training provided: We have a minimum period of full-time training for 2 weeks in an owners store. However, the average training time is 4 to 6 weeks with intensive, one-on-one training both prior to during and after the store opens with continued assistance available on an indefinite basis.

Managerial assistance available: We have a complete management consultant program that includes financing, site location, leasehold improvements, equipment installation, and complete training in ones own store.

The training covers product knowledge, handling, buying, advertising, marketing, ordering, merchandising, pricing, accounting systems, etc., and is available to a buyer on an indefinite basis.

CHEESE SHOP INTERNATIONAL, INC.
25 Amogerone Crossway
Greenwich, Connecticut 06830
Fred D. Walker, Jr., Franchise Administrator

Description of operation: Retail sale of the fine cheese, gourmet foods, related gift items and wines where permissible. Typically located in a shopping center or on Main Street of better suburban communities.

Number of franchisees: 95 in 25 states

In business since: 1965

Equity capital needed: Variable $50,000–$75,000

Financial assistance available: None

Training provided: 4 weeks; 5 days per week actually working in an existing Cheese Shop under the direction of a company expert.

Managerial assistance available: In addition to the training we provide an expert to help during the grand opening week. On a continuous basis we accept collect phone calls to plan and advise on all purchases necessary to run the business. This service includes discussing the following as applies to various suppliers; availability of product, freshness, specials, quality, next arrivals, trucking routes, air freight, costs, etc. It also includes recommending where to place a given order for a certain product at that particular time. This service is optional and typically done on a weekly basis. We also organize promotions, designed to increase sales. Continuous supervision and advice in all phases of retail operations is provided.

WAFFLE KING OF AMERICA, INC.
P.O. Box 2687
Huntington, West Virginia 25726

Description of operation: A complete breakfast menu specializing in waffles and pancakes. Coffee shop atmosphere with sandwiches and full course dinners also served.

Number of franchisees: 4 in West Virginia, Virginia, and Kentucky

In business since: 1973

Equity capital needed: Approximately $25,000

Financial assistance available: No direct financial assistance, however company will assist in preparing all loan applications and assist franchisee with the presentation of the application. Equipment leases have been arranged through private sources.

Training provided: 1-month training program for each franchisee prior to the opening of store, including classroom work and on-the-job training in an existing company store. Company personnel assist at each new location at time of opening.

Managerial assistance available: Never-ending managerial and technical assistance is provided throughout the term of the franchise. Regular visits by company personnel are designed to keep each franchisee up to date with the latest ideas regarding his business and regular management meetings for both company and franchise managers are held.

Foods-Restaurants/Drive-Ins/Carry-Outs

A & W RESTAURANTS, INC.
922 Broadway
Santa Monica, California 90406
Paul Hubert

Description of operation: Drive-in-walk-in restaurants.

Number of franchisees: 1,400 in 44 States

In business since: 1919

Equity capital needed: $50,000 and up

Financial assistance available: Equipment financing available.

Training provided: 2-week training course—mandatory.

Managerial assistance available: Continuous assistance from field personnel.

THE ALL AMERICAN BURGER, INC.
1888 Century Park East,
Suite 214
Los Angeles, California 90067
Howard J. Kastle, Vice President

Description of operation: Fast food restaurants, featuring The All American Burger, salad bars, Mexican food.

Number of franchisees: Over 500 franchises sold throughout the United States and Europe

In business since: 1968

Equity capital needed: $40,000 and up

Financial assistance available: None at present time.

Training provided: Franchisor provides up to 21 days of training in the "All American" methods of operation. In addition, on-location supervision for a period of 48 working hours prior to and after the opening of the restaurant.

Managerial assistance available: Standard plans and specifications for the franchised restaurant are provided to franchisee. Franchisor will administer advertising, public relations, and promotional programs designed to promote and enhance the value of "All American Burger." Continuous supervision of operation at no cost to franchisee. Operations and policy manual plus bookkeeping system provided to the franchisee.

ANCHOR INN RESTAURANTS
5244 Valley Industrial Boulevard
Shakopee, Minnesota 55379

Description of operation: Family-style, waitress served, "all-you-can-eat" restaurants (spirits available).

Number of franchisees: 12 in Minnesota, Wisconsin, Michigan, and California

In business since: 1968

Equity capital needed: Approximately $150,000

Financial assistance available: None

Training provided: Complete managerial program from time of inception to grand opening. Actual on-the-job training of all phases of the individual restaurant.

Managerial assistance available: Managerial program—3–6 weeks. Promotional package—duration of franchise agreement. Use of central purchasing—duration of franchise agreement. Training program—3–6 weeks.

ARMAN'S SYSTEMS, INC.
6165 Central Avenue
Portage, Indiana 46368
Carrol Sarkisian, President

Description of operation: Fast food operation selling hot dogs, hamburgers, tacos, and 53 flavors of ice cream; supplying mixes for taco and chili. Is most successful when owner operated.

Number of franchisees: 13 in Indiana

In business since: 1967

Equity capital needed: $30,000 down, $95,000 total

Financial assistance available: None, franchisee handles own financing. Company builds and leases back.

Training provided: Training on-the-job at our company owned store. Also 2 weeks after restaurant is open with company supervision.

Managerial assistance available: We will be available at all times, any time assistance is needed. We keep a monthly check on percentages to see that they don't get out of line.

AUNT CHILOTTA SYSTEMS, INC.
P.O. Box 1360
Aberdeen, South Dakota 57401
Don Briscoe, President

Description of operation: Limited menu Mexican fast food, featuring carry-out, drive-thru, and inside seating for approximately 30. The restaurant is 28′ × 36′ and it is built on-site. Also available are plans for malls or remodeling existing structures. The total charge, including the franchise fee, is $32,000, and it includes everything needed in the kitchen, from the freezer and refrigerator down to the pans and spoons. Total investment can range from $70,000 to $200,000.

Number of franchisees: 15 in 7 states

In business since: 1976

Equity capital needed: It varies, but generally $25,000 to $50,000.

Financial assistance available: We give information and assistance that should help in securing your own local financing.

Training provided: In a comprehensive 14-day training program you receive on-the-job training in a company-owned restaurant that includes food preparation, product knowledge, inventory, purchasing, portion control, shift scheduling, daily reports, cash register procedures, staff appearance and hygiene, public relations, and success motivation.

Managerial assistance available: One of your operations directors will assist in the actual opening of your new business and on a continuing basis.

We will supply monthly promotions and advertising materials, make periodic inspections, and continue our ongoing research and development to help increase profits.

BAGEL NOSH, INC.
110 East 73rd Street
New York, New York 10021
James McGuirk, Franchise Director

Description of operation: Manufacturing of bagels and sale of delicatessen meats, salads, smoked fish on bagels—no bread used—light hot meals—health salads—cafeteria style with average unit seating 100.

Number of franchisees: 50 in 14 states

In business since: 1973

Equity capital needed: $120,000 cash, including $25,000 franchise fee

Financial assistance available: $275,000 needed to build and equip a Bagel Nosh. Equipment leasing available to qualified individuals. Franchisee may select own bank or SBA.

Training provided: 6 to 8 week mandatory in-store training under supervision of company instructors for all owners, managers, and personnel that franchisee wishes trained.

Managerial assistance available: Bagel Nosh provides continual management service for term of agreement in controls, quality controls. Company supervisors work closely with franchisees and visit all units on regional basis. Operational manuals are provided for all phases of Bagel Nosh operations and standards.

BARNABY'S FAMILY INNS, INC.
2832 West Touhy Avenue
Chicago, Illinois 60645
Charles Hackl

Description of operation: Fast food; self-service. Menu includes pizza, large hamburgers and other hearty sandwiches, beer, and soft drinks. Business is family oriented.

Number of franchisees: 24 in Illinois, Indiana, Missouri, Florida, Virginia, and Wisconsin

In business since: 1968

Equity capital needed: $96,000 minimum

Financial assistance available: None. Franchisee must arrange own financing with our assistance.

Training provided: 4–6 weeks of classroom and on-the-job training.

Managerial assistance available: Assistance is provided for the duration of the contract in areas of operations, marketing, and accounting controls.

BURGER KING CORPORATION
P.O. Box 520783
Miami, Florida 33152
Jeff Seeberger, Vice President, Franchise Development

Description of operation: Limited menu restaurant specializing in hamburgers. Air-conditioned and heated. Seating of 50 to 130 people. Franchises available throughout most of the United States and abroad.

Number of franchisees: More than 2,600 units located in all 50 states, the Bahamas, Puerto Rico, Canada, Spain, Guam, Germany, Sweden, Denmark, England, and Australia

In business since: 1954

Equity capital needed: $110,000, net worth $150,000

Financial assistance available: Franchisee arranges own financing, usually available in local banks and selected national finance or leasing companies.

Training provided: Company operated regional training centers provide extensive and detailed instruction in restaurant operation, equipment, administration for franchisees and/or management.

Managerial assistance available: Operational assistance is provided on an on-going basis as needed through personnel located at regional and district offices operated by Burger King Corporation.

BURGER QUEEN ENTERPRISES, INC.
P.O. Box 6014—4000 DuPont Circle
Louisville, Kentucky 40206
George E. Clark, President

Description of operation: Fast food restaurant.

Number of franchisees: 164 in 7 states; 1 in Canada; 1 in London; 3 in Taipei, Taiwan.

In business since: 1963

Equity capital needed: $50,000 depending upon franchisee's financial capabilities

Financial assistance available: Assistance in acquiring equipment loan or lease. Joint venturing opportunities for qualified candidates.

Training provided: Development training program—5 weeks—combined unit and classroom work at special training unit; follow-up visits at franchisees unit by training director during next 25 weeks and continued visits by area supervisor.

Managerial assistance available: Continued assistance regarding operations and accounting through coordinators and correspondence from home office.

CHICKEN DELIGHT
227 East Sunshine
Suite 119
Springfield, Missouri 65807
Wendell E. Lejeune, Vice President and General Manager

Description of operation: Inside dining and/or carry out and delivery restaurant featuring chicken, shrimp, fish, BBQ ribs, and pizza. Area franchises also available.

Number of franchisees: 130 in 6 states and Canada

In business since: 1952

Equity capital needed: $50,000 to $150,000, depending on size of unit and ability to acquire additional financing

Financial assistance available: None

Training provided: On-the-job training that includes all phases of operations.

Managerial assistance available: Continual assistance in all phases of operations is offered.

CHICKEN MARY'S SYSTEMS, INC.
Box 62489
Pittsburg, Kansas 66762
Larry Zerngast, President

Description of operation: Family style sit-down restaurant specializing in fried chicken with other items on menu. Also interested in joint venture or merger with larger corporation for a large scale operation.

Number of franchisees: 3 in Missouri and Kansas

In business since: 1930

Equity capital needed: $30,000 and up

Financial assistance available: Assistance in funding of land and building; assistance in funding equipment.

Training provided: Training program available for management. Duration of program depends on time required for individual.

Managerial assistance available: Continuous supervisory help.

JAPANESE STEAK HOUSES, INC.
The Maritimes C-22
2051 Northeast Ocean Boulevard
Stuart, Florida 33494
David H. Nelson, President

Description of operation: Own, operate, and franchise by licensee's of Japanese Steak Houses restaurants. The steak houses fit into a free-standing building and build to suit or lease back situations, shopping centers, hotels, and resorts.

Number of franchisees: 24 in 8 states, South Africa, and England.

In business since: 1962

Equity capital needed: Varies between $25,000 to $50,000 depending on marketing area

Financial assistance available: Lease financing, available, if qualified.

Training provided: Extensive training provided.

Managerial assistance available: Continuous training in managerial and technical assistance.

JERRY'S RESTAURANTS
JERRICO, INC.
P.O. Box 11988
Lexington, Kentucky 40579
Ernie Renaud, Executive Vice President

Description of operation: Coffee shops and dining room operations. Family oriented, informal. Located in cities over 10,000. Interstate locations and in conjunction with motels. We will franchise on a selected basis and limited areas.

Number of franchisees: 70 in Kentucky, Tennessee, Ohio, Indiana, and Florida

In business since: 1929

Equity capital needed: $100,000

Financial assistance available: None

Training provided: Complete training course for management. Opening assistance in the form of traveling supervisory crew.

Managerial assistance available: Continued supervision program through field consultants.

JIFFY JOINTS, INC.
216 Capital National Bank Building
Austin, Texas 78701
Curtiss Ryan, President

Description of operation: A specialty hot dog stand franchise featuring Jiffy Franks the "burpless" hot dog served in a special bun with a toasted hole in it to prevent the usual mess of eating a hot dog. Jiffy Franks were developed in 1971 and previously were sold only through theaters in the Southwest. The product leaves no after taste, does not cause indigestion or heartburn, and does not shrink or shrivel when heated.

Number of franchisees: 3 in Texas

In business since: 1978

Equity capital needed: $10,000–$25,000

Financial assistance available: Equipment package financing available. Also $5,000 franchise fee financing available. Assistance in site selection.

Training provided: 1-week supervised training. Inventory control, daily reports, and continuous operations assistance.

Managerial assistance available: Certified public accountant monthly profit and loss statements prepared at cost to franchisees. Continuous point of sale material and advertising promotions coordinated from the franchisor.

KENNEY'S FRANCHISE CORP.
1602 Midland Road
Salem, Virginia 24153
William Kenney, President

Description of operation: Fast food. Hamburgers, pressure fried chicken, and other related food items.

Number of franchisees: 4 in Virginia, West Virginia, and Florida

In business since: 1958

Equity capital needed: $10,000 franchise fee, $70,000 equipment, and $10,000 working capital.

Financial assistance available: Not at this time

Training provided: 2 week—total operation. Assistance by key personnel on opening.

Managerial assistance available: 2-week training at home office. Supervision for 1 week. Thereafter one visit per month or more often if required.

KEN'S PIZZA PARLORS, INC.
4441 South 72nd East Avenue
Tulsa, Oklahoma 74145
Michael E. Bartlett, Vice President

Description of operation: The Ken's Pizza Parlor concept entails an integrated system utilizing an attractive free-standing building with a drive-thru window, a unique limited menu and a simplified operating concept. Taken all together, the system combines a profitable menu with comfortable table service format.

Number of franchisees: 26—a total of 166 locations (62 company owned) in 14 states

In business since: 1961

Equity capital needed: Initial franchise fee—$10,000. Land, building, and equipment must be financed by franchisee.

Financial assistance available: None

Training provided: Training program provided in Tulsa, Oklahoma training store. Program is extensive and follows a formal "management training" manual. Time required varies between 4–12 weeks depending upon capabilities and previous experience of licensee.

Managerial assistance available: Three full-time employees travel among franchise stores offering operational assistance, further training, and inspections. Company regularly conducts new product and training seminars in its Tulsa facilities. All franchisees are invited to these seminars. Company also provides confidential training manual.

KFC CORPORATION
P.O. Box 32070
Louisville, Kentucky 40232
Rebecca Enders, Manager, Franchising Department

Description of operation: Sale of Colonel Sanders' Kentucky Fried Chicken and related products.

Number of franchisees: 720 in all states except Montana, Utah, and Florida

In business since: March 1964 (purchase of Kentucky Fried Chicken, Inc., which was begun in 1952 by Colonel Harland Sanders.)

Equity capital needed: Variable. $4,000 initial franchise fee. Land, building, and equipment must be financed by franchisee.

Financial assistance available: None

Training provided: Required of all new franchisees and recommended for key employees: 12-day training seminar covering proper store operation including management, accounting, sales, advertising, catering, and purchasing. Ongoing training provided in areas of customer service, general restaurant management, and quality control. Also available: sales hostess instruction and seminars for instruction on specific KFC programs and equipment such as the automatic cooker. Franchisees are also provided with confidential operating manual.

LORDBURGER SYSTEMS, INC.
3690 Orange Place
Suite 521
Beachwood, Ohio 44122
Louis A. Frangos, Executive Vice President

Description of operation: Lordburger Systems, Inc., owns/operates and directs a successful chain of fast service family restaurants, serving moderately priced menu. Emphasis is placed on, quick, efficient service, high quality food and superior cleanliness standards. Menus consists of Lordburger's famous ground round hamburger. Hamburgers, cheeseburgers, fish sandwiches, ham & cheese sandwiches, french fries, shakes, ice cream sundaes, extended breakfast menu, and assorted hot and cold beverages.

Number of franchisees: 24 in Ohio

In business since: 1971

Equity capital needed: $85,000 to $95,000 and the ability to obtain financing for $110,000 minimum

Training provided: Lordburger provides a thorough comprehensive 300-hour, on-the-job, training program. This 300 hours is comprised of an orientation 2-week basic operations course, and 2 weeks of additional advanced management training course at the Lordburger Training Center, the balance of training is conducted in a Lordburger Restaurant.

Managerial assistance available: Lordburger Systems, Inc., provides operations, training, maintenance, and equipment manuals. Also provided are personnel management, quality control, and purchasing programs. In addition the company makes available promotional advertising and marketing materials, plus field operations representative for consultation and operational assistance.

LOSURDO FOODS, INC.
20 Owens Road
Hackensack, New Jersey 07601
Michael Losurdo, President

Description of operation: Italian restaurant with accent on pizza

Number of franchisees: 10 in New York, New Jersey, Pennsylvania, North Carolina, and Florida

Equity capital needed: $25,000

Financial assistance available: None

Training provided: 2 week training period plus regular monthly training session.

Managerial assistance available: Continual assistance in product preparation and advertising assistance.

LOVE'S WOOD PIT BARBEQUE RESTAURANTS
6837 Lankershim Boulevard
North Hollywood, California 91605
Bob R. Leonard, Vice President—Franchise Operations

Description of operation: Complete full service barbeque restaurant featuring zesty barbequed ribs, beef, pork, and chicken. Love's is a medium-priced lunch and dinner house located in the western United States. Love's restaurants are open for lunch, dinner and late evening suppers. Most offer cocktail lounge service.

Number of franchisees: 31 in Arizona, California, Colorado, Oregon, Washington (new units restricted to Southern California)

Equity capital needed: $60,000 franchise fee plus financing of land, building, and equipment.

Financial assistance available: None

Training provided: 4 weeks classroom and on-the-job instruction.

Managerial assistance available: Franchisor provides opening supervision, assists in hiring of personnel plus regular visits and assistance from field coordinators. Complete manual of operations specifies how each menu item is prepared and served, how the business may be operated effectively.

MARTIN'S FRANCHISING SYSTEMS, INC.
6096 Gordon Road
Marbleton, Georgia 30059
Ray L. Martin, President

Description of operation: Fast food restaurant with drive-thru, car service, and inside seating facilities. We specialize in a chicken filet sandwich and other specialty items.

Number of franchisees: 3 in Georgia

In business since: 1962; Martin's Franchising System since 1979

Equity capital needed: $30,000 total. $10,000 working capital, $10,000 franchise fee, and $10,000 equipment down payment

Financial assistance available: Assistance in obtaining equipment financing (full package $80,000).

Training provided: On-the-job training for 2 weeks prior to startup; 2 weeks after startup, plus any further assistance necessary for duration of contract.

Managerial assistance available: We provide the same as above for management personnel plus an operating manual along with periodic inspections and continuous monitoring of records for possible problems. We are involved in every aspect of the business.

MCDONALD'S CORPORATION
1 McDonald's Plaza
Oak Brook, Illinois 60521
Licensing Manager

Description of operation: McDonald's Corporation operates and directs a successful nationwide chain of fast food restaurants serving moderately priced menu. Emphasis is on quick, efficient service, high quality food, and cleanliness. The standard menu consists of hamburgers, cheeseburgers, fish sandwiches, french fries, apple pie, shakes, breakfast menu, and assorted beverages.

Number of franchisees: 4,859 in the United States, 890 internationally (including Canada)

In business since: 1955

Equity capital needed: $125,000 minimum and ability to acquire outside financing $125,000 to $200,000

Financial assistance available: None

Training provided: Minimum of 200 hours preregistration and 300 plus postregistration; 11 days of basic operations training and 2 weeks managerial training at Hamburger University in Elk Grove, Illinois.

Managerial assistance available: Operations, training, maintenance, accounting, and equipment manuals provided. Company makes available promotional advertising material plus field representative consultation and assistance.

General Merchandising Stores

BEN FRANKLIN
DIVISION CITY PRODUCTS CORPORATION
1700 South Wolf Road
Des Plaines, Illinois 60018
L. V. Dambis, Vice President Franchise and Real Estate Development

Description of operation: Ben Franklin Stores is a general merchandise operation. This division of City Products Corporation provides both merchandise and retailing assistance to franchisees in all 50 states. The franchise operates a private business with the advantages of chain-store buying, merchandising, and promotional guidance, and a nationwide reputation for professional service to the public.

Number of franchisees: 1,700 in 50 states

In business since: 1877

Equity capital needed: Minimum of $80,000

Financial assistance available: Financing is arranged through local and regional commercial institutions.

Training provided: Training provided for franchisee and employees in selected stores by trained field personnel and store manager. Duration is flexible (usually 30 days) depending upon background, qualifications, and needs of franchised owner.

Managerial assistance available: Assistance is available in finding locations, sales promotion, and all phases of operation by periodic visits of field and headquarters personnel.

RASCO STORES
Division of GAMBLE-SKOGMO, INC.
2777 North Ontario Street
Burbank, California 91504
Franchise Personnel Manager

Description of operation: Rasco Stores offer two types of franchises: Rasco Variety (a family store) and Toy World (toy specialty stores).

Number of franchisees: 20 in 4 states

In business since: 1934

Equity capital needed: Minimum down payment: Rasco Variety $50,000; Toy World $5,000 to $80,000

Financial assistance available: Franchisee, after initial down payment, may have the remainder of his indebtedness financed by Rasco Stores unless he prefers to arrange outside financing.

Training provided: 2 to 3 days basic indoctrination in Burbank, California office. Balance of training in the franchisee's store under the supervision of the district manager.

Managerial assistance available: Rasco Stores offer mass buying power, modern merchandising ideas, complete accounting services, store layout and opening assistance, advertising program. Store building rental plan, fixture rental plan, and operating assistance by district managers and buyers.

Health Aids/Services

ALPHA NURSES
909 Burnett Street
Wichita Falls, Texas 76301
J. D. Popejoy, Franchise Director

Description of operation: Alpha Nurses is an *employer* of nursing and health care personnel and other paramedical personnel, which are made available to the growing market of geriatrics, postoperative, cardiacs, pediatrics, and other convalescents in the privacy of their home, hospital, and health-related facilities.

Number of franchisees: 3 in Texas and Arizona

In business since: 1978

Equity capital needed: From $20,000 to $30,000 depending on location

Financial assistance available: Accounts receivable financing as needed.

Training provided: Mandatory 3-week on-site training, plus 1-week on-site training as follow-up, as needed.

Managerial assistance available: Alpha provides continual management service for the life of the franchise in such areas as bookkeeping, advertising, inventory control. Complete manuals of operations, forms, and directions are provided. District and field managers are available in all regions to work closely with franchisees regularly to assist solving problems. Alpha sponsors meetings of franchisees and conducts marketing and service research to maintain high Alpha consumer acceptance.

Lawn and Garden Supplies/Services

LAWN-A-MAT CHEMICAL AND EQUIPMENT CORPORATION
54 Kinkel Street
Westbury, New York 11590

Description of operation: Lawn service and products for the home owner, offering a wide range of products and services.

Number of franchisees: 155 in 15 states

In business since: 1961

Equity capital needed: $3,500

Financial assistance available: For qualified applicants.

Training provided: Primary training at franchisor's centers.

Managerial assistance available: Agronomical, managerial, technical, and sales training provided on a continuing basis at regular seminars and in the field. Personnel available to solve special problems.

Hotels/Motels

FAMILY INNS OF AMERICA, INC.
P.O. Box 10
Pigeon Forge, Tennessee 37863
Kenneth M. Seaton, President

Description of operation: Motels with food and beverage facilities.

Number of franchisees: 34 in 10 states

In business since: 1971

Equity capital needed: Between $100,000 and $250,000 depending upon size desired

Financial assistance available: Feasibility studies, plans, guidance and counseling with financial institutions, national contracts for lower construction cost. Investment opportunities thru limited partnerships.

Training provided: Complete training; covering all phases of motel business, room renting, restaurant and lounge set-up, and planning as long as needed.

Managerial assistance available: Guidance and counseling on company policies, complete audit and accounting forms. Complete inspections by company, annual meetings, and other help will be given at any time.

HAPPY INNS OF AMERICA, INC.
8849 Richmond Highway
Alexandria, Virginia 22309
Clark S. Morris, President

Description of operation: Franchisor of motor inns.

Number of franchisees: 20 in 7 states

In business since: 1970

Equity capital needed: Approximately 20 percent of construction cost

Financial assistance available: Will assist in preparing the presenting mortgage package to financial institutions

Training provided: 30-days training for managers on-job; continued supervision throughout life of contract; operation manual, continually updated.

Managerial assistance available: Continual management assistance as needed.

HOLIDAY INNS, INC.
3796 Lamar Avenue
Memphis, Tennessee 38118
Laurence Parry, Vice President, Franchise Operations

Description of operation: Hotels and restaurants.

Number of franchisees: 1,510 franchises worldwide and 1,748 Holiday Inns worldwide

In business since: 1954

Equity capital needed: Varies depending on the size of the project

Financial assistance available: None

Training provided: 3-week course at Holiday Inn University.

Managerial assistance available: Continuing guidance as needed.

Pet Shops

DOCKTOR PET CENTERS, INC.
Dundee Park
Andover, Massachusetts 01810
Leslie Charm, President
Eugene H. Kohn, Vice President

Description of operation: Retail pets, supplies, and pet accessories.

Number of franchisees: 72 franchises operating in 142 stores in 31 states

In business since: 1966

Equity capital needed: Approximately $60,000 to $75,000

Financial assistance available: Yes, in certain cases

Training provided: 3 weeks at franchisor's headquarters, subjects covered include store operations, care and maintenance of pets, accounting, management, inventory, maintenance, personnel selection, merchandising, etc.

Managerial assistance available: Advise on stocking, fixture arrangement, receipt of livestock, maintenance procedures, and profit control, etc. On-the-site advisor guides franchisee during first 2 weeks of operations. Advertising materials, accounting forms, and seasonal signs furnished. Counselors make frequent visits to stores to assist franchisees.

FLYING FUR PET TRAVEL SERVICE
310 South Michigan Avenue
Chicago, Illinois 60604
R. I. Fredriksen, National Manager

Description of operation: Animal shipping U.S.A.–overseas, with pickup and delivery service, vaccination certificates, animal boarding on stopovers or delay in transit program. Coast-to-coast network includes and provides veterinarian, animal hospital and clinic, grooming. Includes documentation and moving-storage coordination. Traveling kennels available.

Number of franchisees: 15 in 10 states

In business since: 1970

Equity capital needed: $500

Financial assistance available: None

Training provided: 2 to 3 initial meetings and follow-up as needed.

Managerial assistance available: As Needed.

PEDIGREE PET CENTERS, DIV. OF
PEDIGREE INDUSTRIES, INC.
11 Goldthwait Road
Marblehead, Massachusetts 01945
Milton Docktor, President

Description of operation: Retail pets, supplies, accessories, and grooming services.

Number of franchisees: 4 in Maine, Massachusetts, Florida, and New Jersey

In business since: 1975—Predecessor in business since 1927

Equity capital needed: Approximately $40,000

Financial assistance available: Franchisor may assist in obtaining financing.

Training provided: 4 weeks at franchisor's headquarters. Covers store operation, care of pets, accounting, management, inventory, maintenance, and personnel selection.

Managerial assistance available: Advice on stocking, fixture arrangement, receipt of livestock, and maintenance procedures. On-the-site advisor guides franchisee during first week of operations. Advertising materials and standardized accounting and report forms furnished. Counselors make visits to stores to assist franchisees.

PETLAND, INC.
195 North Hickory Street
P.O. Box 1606
Chillicothe, Ohio 45601
Edward R. Kunzelman, President

Description of operation: Retail pets, pet supplies, and pet-related items; grooming services.

Number of franchisees: 38 plus 5 company-owned stores in 10 states and Canada

In business since: 1967

Equity capital needed: $15,000 to $30,000, depending on store size and location

Financial assistance available: Franchisor may finance a portion of the cost and will also assist in preparation of financial presentation package.

Training provided: 4 weeks in operating stores as assigned, and classroom at Ohio main office or Florida office. Additional assistance in-store after opening.

Managerial assistance available: Assistance in merchandising, livestock management, and maintenance procedures. On-the-site advisor guides franchisee during first week of operations. Advertising materials and standardized accounting and report forms furnished. Area field supervisors make periodic visits and inspections and will give assistance in problem areas. Advertising manual, operations manual, counter reference book, and all forms and guarantees for operations are provided.

PET MASTER, INC.
4161 Southwest 6th Street
Ft. Lauderdale, Florida 33317
Jack Vander Plate, President

Description of operation: Pet Master, Inc., is a mobile pet grooming service. The franchise includes an air conditioned step van fully equipped to bathe, dip, and groom all dog breeds in its fully contained mobile unit in the customer's driveway. Also carried is a full supply of pet needs and grooming supplies.

Number of franchisees: 6 in Florida

In business since: 1973

Equity capital needed: $7,000 to $10,000

Financial assistance available: Mobile van can be financed on a 5-year lease or 5-year bank loan.

Training provided: 5 weeks of training at company's training center Ft. Lauderdale, Florida. Courses include breed identification, dog handling, art of grooming, bookkeeping, and customer relations. Five weeks training with experienced groomer in your mobile van in your own franchise territory. Continuous assistance in every phase of business.

Managerial assistance available: Pet Master provides continual management service for the life of the franchise in such areas as advertising, public relations, and new ideas and products in the industry.

Real Estate

ACTION BROKERS CORPORATION
5001 West 80th Street
Bloomington, Minnesota 55437
Richard O. Watland, President

Description of operation: Real estate sales.

Number of franchisees: 10 in Minnesota

In business since: 1975

Equity capital needed: $5,000

Financial assistance available: Local financing

Training provided: Prelicense classes and training classes and management.

Managerial assistance available: All experienced brokers and licensed with the state prior to obtaining a franchise.

BETHOM CORPORATION
BETTER HOMES REALTY
675 Ygnacio Valley Road, Suite A202
Walnut Creek, California 94596
Ernest H. Ewan, President

Description of operation: Bethom Corporation, dba Better Homes Realty, is principally engaged in the business of franchising real estate sales offices.

Number of franchisees: 300 in California

In business since: 1969

Equity capital needed: $6,500

Financial assistance available: None

Training provided: Total management and salesman orientation; continued management assistance; on-going educational seminars.

Managerial assistance available: Total management and salesman orientation; continued management assistance; on-going educational seminars.

EMBASSY RENTAL AGENCY
P.O. Box 706
Orange, New Jersey 07051
George Livieratos, President

Description of operation: Embassy Rental Agency is a full real estate service specializing in apartment and home rentals.

Number of franchisees: 3 in New Jersey

In business since: 1963

Equity capital needed: $10,000 minimum

Financial assistance available: As long as party is qualified, franchisor will help financing.

Training provided: Full training in our home office as long as is necessary for franchisee to succeed.

Managerial assistance available: Constant support while in training, with continuing support from main company.

EXECU-SYSTEMS, INC.
727 East Maryland
Phoenix, Arizona 85014
Mark Lestikow, National Marketing Manager

Description of operation: National franchisor for the original 100 percent concept. Execu-Systems is designed to assist individuals and entities in the development of strong, multi-office companies operating general real estate brokerages using the Execu-Systems 100 percent concept as the foundation.

Number of franchisees: 67 offices in 23 states

In business since: 1965

Equity capital needed: $7,500 licensing fee; minimum of $15,000–$20,000

Financial assistance available: None

Training provided: Intensive 2-day workshop, given by national staff, instructing new member how to own and operate the Execu-Systems 100 percent concept using methods with 15 years of proven success. A 300-page operations manual, coupled with accessibility of a national staff, who also administer company owned offices, provide on-going assistance. A regional consultant program is also provided where applicable. Program assists new member in early phases of operation.

Managerial assistance available: Unlimited consultation in proven successful accounting process, recruiting, secretarial hiring, and advertising methods is provided. National and regional meetings cover topics of vital interest to members. Operation of national referral service and volume purchasing available to member brokers and their associates.

Index